The Counseling Handbook

The
Counseling
Handbook

Practical Strategies
to Help Children with
Common Problems

Nancy Flood & Maureen Nuckols

CALL 1·800·962·1141

The Counseling Handbook

By Nancy Flood and Maureen Nuckols
Jacket and book design by Patti Eslinger
Jacket illustration by Frank Renlie

Childswork/Childsplay publishes products for mental health professionals, teachers and parents who wish to help children with their developmental, social and emotional growth. For questions, comments, or to request a free catalog describing hundreds of games, toys, books, and other counseling tools, call 1-800-962-1141.

© 1998 Childswork/Childsplay
A Brand of The Guidance Group
www.guidance-group.com

ISBN 10: 1-882732-65-0
ISBN 13: 978-1-882732-65-4

*To our women's group: Karen Gerbaz, Sue Maisch, Debbie McKenna,
and Nancy Reinisch—what can we say but so many thanks for friendship and
for adding laughter to tears.*

Acknowledgements

We are grateful to our families for reading and rereading this manuscript and for their encouragement and patience. With big hugs to Mark, Adam, and Aaron and to Bill, Megan, Michael, Elizabeth, and Macey. You said we could do it, and we believed you.

Special thanks to the people at Northern Marianas College on the Pacific Island of Saipan, especially to President Agnes McPhetres, who models the courage and caring of a true educator.

Contents

Preface

Counseling children is usually an intense and often varied experience. This morning, for example, I was on my hands and knees playing puppets with a nonverbal three-year-old who had been abandoned and placed in foster care; this afternoon I sat across from an expressionless teenager who had lost 35 pounds in the last nine months. Because I am forced to switch gears so many times a day, I sometimes wonder which treatment strategy to try first.

Often I need practical information. Many times after a young client has left, I have rushed to scan my bookshelf in search of answers to questions such as: What else should I ask? What other information do I need? How can I elicit that information from the child or parent? What should I do during therapy with the child, during talks with the parents, during consultation with the teachers? What treatment goals are reasonable? What have I forgotten? How do I answer parents who ask why this happened, what can they do at home, or how they can help?

This book was written to help you—the counselor or therapist—treat children. It provides practical and concise information, emphasizing treatment rather than diagnosis. It is formatted as a handbook so that you can easily select the appropriate topic and quickly find the information you need. Each chapter begins with an overview of the problem along with important social, cultural, and statistical information. Next, assessment and diagnosis are briefly reviewed, with descriptions of children's concerns, fears, and hopes and explanations of their behavioral responses to these concerns. Each chapter also addresses developmental considerations—key variables at each developmental stage that affect the child's ability to adjust, followed by a thorough discussion of intervention strategies, including cognitive and behavioral strategies for you, the counselor; specific therapeutic interventions parents can try; and suggestions for teachers. The progress and outcomes you can expect are outlined, along with the most frequent reasons for poor therapeutic progress. A directory of resources for parents, teachers, counselors, and children concludes each chapter.

The books listed in the bibliographies were carefully selected; bibliotherapy can be a vital element in the therapeutic process. Sometimes one book makes all the difference. Books can diminish fears and connect children to other children who have similar worries and concerns. Books can also connect children to other adults, providing a safe forum for talking about "the kid in the book" who is having similar troubles. A good book can extend your advice, techniques, and support. In therapy you have a child for only an hour or less a week. A parent told me recently, "I can't believe how often my son pulls out that book on stepfamilies you recommended." A good book has more authority and "believability," especially with older children, than any adult's words. Books can be a critical, vital part of treatment.

Working with children and families is difficult, sometimes heartbreaking work. Our hope, as coauthors and therapists, is that when you reach for this book, you will find a practical guide that makes your job easier and more fulfilling.

Maureen Nuckols and Nancy Flood

November 1997

CHAPTER 1

Divorce

It was the end of the therapy session. Aaron blew out the candle.

"Did you make a wish?" I asked.

"I wished that Mom and Dad would never be divorced, never, and we all live together forever and ever." Aaron looked up at me. "Will my wish still come true even though I told it?"

Divorce is the most common trauma encountered by American children. In 1994, 40% of children in the United States were living in divorced families. An equal number were living in single, remarried, or "blended" families. The American reality is that a significant number of children experience the effects of divorce. The stigma of having a divorced family is not as distressing as it once was, but the trauma experienced by children has not diminished.

Divorce is an experience of loss. For children, it means dealing with confusion, conflict, change, anger, and sadness while struggling with the challenges of growing up. Divorce often means losing a parent, changing schools or neighborhoods, sharing parents, adding new family members, or watching a parent date an "intruder." Meanwhile, children still need to be children and must cope with school issues, friends, activities, sports, and so on.

Understanding and adjusting to divorce is a developmental process. There are stages of healing for children just as there are stages of recovery for parents. The timing and pace of children's healing are directly linked to their growth and development. As children's thinking matures, they gain new understanding of their parents' divorce. This deepening awareness means re-experiencing the losses, and so the divorce continues to affect them. The child who was three when his or her parents divorced may revis-it the events and trauma of the divorce when adolescence begins. The parents, for whom the divorce is long over, may be surprised and caught off guard. It is difficult for the parents to understand their child's new aware-ness and renewed anger and pain.

However, parents and their children can weather divorce and emerge healthy. A child's adjustment depends on many factors, the most important of which is the parents' recovery. In her book *Second Chances*, Judith Wallerstein identifies the two most powerful variables affecting children's adjustment—the mental health of the primary parent and the quality of par-enting during and after divorce.

This is encouraging information. If the adults can actively parent their children through the many family changes that are part of any divorce and maintain their own emotional health, children can be protected from long-term emotional harm. As a counselor, you can effectively assist parents and children during this turbulent time of transition. Your role as counselor is multifaceted. It involves providing divorce education, furthering communi-cation between family members, guiding appropriate emotional expression, supporting behavioral management strategies, and often mediating critical family issues.

ASSESSMENT

Assess the family's history of interaction. Did healthy patterns of trust, car-ing, and communication once exist? To understand the marital and divorce history of the family, interview both of the parents and the children—the parents separately from their children. Each member of the family will have a different experience; each will have his or her own perspective and under-standing about the reasons for the divorce.

Diagnostic Criteria

Although the divorce of parents often presents a crisis for children, there is no specific diagnosis to describe all the behavioral and emotional reactions of children. However, the diagnosis of Adjustment Disorder is appropriate to portray the variety of symptoms experienced by children of divorce. The critical components of an adjustment disorder are an identifiable stressor—such as the divorce of parents—and significant behavioral impairment, which could include regression, aggressive behaviors, and loss of interest in school.

Additional diagnostic options or descriptors include:

- depression (the child feels hopeless and sad)
- anxiety (the child fears separation from either parent and is afraid of being abandoned)
- mixed anxiety and depression
- disturbance of conduct (the child exhibits common misbehaviors, such as fighting, truancy, shoplifting, or academic withdrawal)

The diagnosis of Adjustment Disorder is short-term by definition and hopeful in prognosis. The emphasis is on adjusting or healing. Also, in this era of open information and lack of privacy, the diagnosis of Adjustment Disorder has practical value; it carries the most benign label.

Behavioral Indicators

For children younger than six, the most common behavioral indicator is regression, a "stepping backwards," or losing developmental progress. For older children, the most common reason for counseling referrals is misbehavior. For example, a child may show aggressive behavior with friends or family members, especially with the custodial parent. Teachers often report slips in academic performance.

Assessment Tools

Projective techniques allow children to make honest responses about topics they may otherwise find too threatening. The underlying assumption in these methods is that children will project their inner selves onto a drawing, an incomplete sentence, or a sand tray creation, or through puppet or dollhouse play. The familiarity of the situation and the indirectness of the expression make these tasks safe and manageable for the child. The opportunity to use actions, especially play actions, rather than words, allows most children to be emotionally expressive.

Drawing is a favorite technique of most school-aged children. This task is especially valuable for young children who have limited vocabularies. Ask children to DRAW-A-PERSON, to draw their family doing something (KINETIC FAMILY DRAWING), and to draw a HOUSE-TREE-PERSON.

The first step in evaluating a drawing is to note your overall impression. Is the drawing big and confident or small, with few details? Is it organized or chaotic? Look, for example, at the placement of figures (i.e., which family members are close to the child?); at the organization of the picture (i.e., how are individuals grouped?); at whether significant figures are omitted (i.e., is the father missing?); and at whether unusual elements are included (i.e., does the picture include a parent the child has not seen for two years?). Be sure to ask the child to tell you all about the drawing.

The DRAW-A-PERSON drawing gives information about a child's view of self. The KINETIC FAMILY DRAWING provides insight into children's feelings, hopes, or wishes about their family. In blended families, the child often has trouble figuring out where to put everyone, and whom to include or exclude. *Children Draw and Tell* by Klepsch and Logie provides interpretations of children's drawings. *Draw-A-Person: A Quantitative Scoring System,* another valuable resource, is available through mail-order catalogs that specialize in psychologically oriented products.

Another projective tool is the rosebush visualization and drawing. This technique provides a window into a child's internal world. The therapist asks the child to visualize a rosebush—to imagine its flowers, leaves, roots, or thorns. Where are they growing? Is anything near or far? What season is it? What kind of day or evening is it? The child should be instructed to draw a picture of what was imagined and to tell a story about the rosebush. In *Inscapes of a Child's World,* John Allen describes post-drawing inquiry and analysis.

As another option or in addition to drawing, the INCOMPLETE SENTENCE provides simple sentence stems that facilitate further discussion.

Make sure the stems include:

• My dad/My mom. . .

• I wish my family. . .

- The best thing about my family is. . .
- I worry/I am afraid. . .
- One thing that no one knows about my family is. . .

     For stepfamily issues use:

- My stepfather/stepmother is. . .
- I can tell my stepmother/stepfather is angry when. . .
- One thing I don't like about my stepmother/stepfather is. . .

Provide a model by answering a few questions yourself. If the child is not adept at reading or writing, be the "secretary." Try to make using this technique fun, like a game.

In conjunction with these projective techniques, the Reynolds Child Depression Inventory—a straightforward, easily administered test to evaluate the severity of a child's depressive symptoms—is valuable in the general assessment of children of divorce. The questions are written at a second-grade level. They can be read to the younger child or to a child who does not read, and the child can answer orally.

Key Issues to Explore

How long have the parents been physically separated? For children, this usually marks the "real" beginning of the divorce; children's emotional reactions to divorce begin when separation occurs.

What is the emotional atmosphere surrounding the divorce? During the critical time of initial separation, did the parents keep concerns about the children a priority? Which parent wanted or initiated the divorce?

What type of relationship do the parents have now? Specifically, are the parents cooperative with each other? Can they communicate and compromise about critical issues such as visitation schedules, shared responsibilities, and finances?

What has changed as a result of the divorce? Ask whether the children have changed residence, school, day care, or friendships. Also ask about losses of private space (bedroom), pets, after-school activities, and "family time." How has the children's daily routine been altered because of the changes in their parents' lives?

Has a new relationship developed for either parent? If so, check on the timing of this relationship and its impact on the amount of shared time with, and attention to, the children. Also ask whether the new partner has children and, if so, whether they are involved in visits and activities.

What factors influenced the ending of the marriage? Were there such problems as physical, emotional, or sexual abuse; verbal or physical fighting between adults; alcohol or drug abuse; infidelity?

How has the divorce changed each parent's financial status? Is either parent working a second job or longer hours?

Who has legal custody? What is the visitation schedule, and is it working? How far away both in physical and emotional distance is each parent from the children?

Developmental Considerations

Often parents ask, "When is the best time for us to divorce—now, or when the children are older?"

There is not a best or worst time for divorce to happen in a child's life. Each developmental stage a child experiences encompasses certain vulnerabilities that are related to the child's emotional and social tasks. While adjusting to the many losses of divorce, a child is also trying to master the "kid tasks" of growing up and learning—learning to walk, read, ride a bike, and make friends.

The Developmental Issues Chart on page 7 summarizes children's emotional tasks, the usual behavioral and emotional signs of stress for each developmental stage, and appropriate intervention. It is important that a counselor understand not only the normal developmental tasks for each stage but also how children in each stage respond to stress.

The key developmental task of the infant and toddler is to form a primary attachment and learn to trust. Stability, consistency, and having a secure home base are essential. Children this young have only a few ways to show stress and upset. However, they are sensitive to family tension and unhappiness. Infants and toddlers show stress by regressing. Parents will

Table 1.1 **Developmental Issues Chart**

	Developmental Tasks	Response to Divorce/Separation	Interventions
Infants and Toddlers	• Formation of primary attachment • Learning to trust	• Regression • Infants—fussy • Toddlers—whiny and clingy	• Help parents create a secure home base and predictable routine
Preschool (2-1/2 -5 years)	• Egocentric thinking • Independence • Ability to separate	• Regression in developmental steps • Expression of feelings through behavior • Aggressive behavior	• Introduce play therapy to help the child express grief, fears, and anger • Teach displacement to parents • Reinforce predictable routines
Early Elementary (6-8 years)	• Competence and mastery • Branching from family	• Drop in academic performance • Depressive symptoms, new fears, nightmares, fear of losing parent	• Teach language of feelings. • Help child create a worry/fear list and a "how to fix it" plan with parents • Teach displacement communication
Late Elementary (9-12 years)	• Competence and mastery • Black-and-white sense of fairness	• Loyalty split between parents • Misbehavior, academic withdrawal • Possible role reversal with parent	• Teach safe ways to express anger • Teach relaxation exercises • Build on child's strengths • Include parent-child sessions
Adolescence	• Independence/separation • Search for identity	• Emancipation from family may be accelerated or delayed • Possible substance use	• Focus directly on adolescent's world and goals.

notice changes in sleep, eating, or elimination patterns. Babies may become fussy and toddlers may become more negative, whiny, and clingy. The counselor can help the parents recognize the importance of keeping a secure and calm home base and a predictable routine. Even if children this young don't understand what is happening to the family, they can sense that the emotional climate of the family is tense and unhappy.

Preschool children will also process and express their feelings about separation and divorce through their behavior. Remember, this is the stage of egocentric thinking; the child feels like the cause of everything that happens. A preschooler will think, I made my parents fight. I made Dad go away and Mom cry. Parents will see a child's regression in toilet training, sleep, language, independence, and ability to separate; they may even see regression in motor skills. The preschool teacher may report aggressive behavior toward other children. Talk with parents about the changes they have observed in their children's behavior.

Six- to eight-year-old children are beginning to branch out from the family. Focused on the tasks of competency and mastery, they are reading, playing sports, riding bicycles, and making friends, whom they may prefer to be with over family. The divorce of their parents can temporarily distract children from these tasks. A withdrawal from childlike activities or a drop in school attendance or performance is often a warning to parents that the stress of divorce is interfering. Children this age express feelings—including feelings of sadness, worry, fear, or anger—more verbally and directly. However, children whose parents are divorcing may indirectly express their emotions by experiencing new bedtime fears or nightmares about people they love getting lost or hurt. They may develop school phobia, which is usually a fear of leaving a parent, or begin to fear such things as monsters and disasters, which represent ways of losing people they love.

There is a definite shift in children's reactions during the later elementary school years, ages 9 to 12. This age group is more idealistic and has a strong black-and-white sense of fairness. These children demand explanations for what is happening to their families. Their loyalty may be split between parents, and they may decide one is right and one is wrong. Misbehavior, negativity, academic withdrawal, noncompliance to rules at home, or using role reversal with a parent are some of the behavioral indicators for counseling.

Adolescence is normally a time for independence, a search for identity, and separation. Divorce can push a child out of the family prematurely, causing him or her to become overly involved with dating and sexuality. Or the opposite may also occur: a child may take over the responsibilities of an absent parent, withdraw from normal adolescent activities, and delay emancipation.

INTERVENTION STRATEGIES
What Counselors Can Do

As the counselor, your first goal is to establish a counseling relationship with the child that is nonbiased, confidential, and nonjudgmental. Within this safe environment, the child can ask any questions and express feelings without worrying that you will get mad, feel hurt, tell the parents, or take sides. Ideally, you can meet with both parents to stress the child's privacy and explain that your focus is understanding the child's experience. It is helpful if both adults support the counseling process. Although sometimes only phone contact with the noncustodial parent is possible, it is essential that the parents hear from you that you are neutral and respectful, and that you will be working as the child's counselor and advocate. For your own financial protection, have a clear understanding from the beginning with both parents about who is responsible for paying your fees.

In *Second Chances,* Wallerstein describes seven tasks that children confront as they react and respond to divorce. These are listed below, followed by recommended counseling strategies:

Task 1. *Children must come to acknowledge that the divorce is happening and that their family is changing.*

Strategy. Discuss in practical terms how the family is changing. Ask about who lives with whom, where, and when. Encourage the child to explain how long the new living arrangements have existed, how long they will continue, who made the plans, and how the new schedule feels. With complicated visitation schedules, often a calendar or a picture chart will help everyone understand the living-visitation schedule. Ask the child to describe where he or she will sleep at each home and how the homes are similar and different. As children describe the basic living arrangements, they learn ways to describe what they are experiencing and how they feel about these changes. For example, Jenny, seven years old, was able to identify quickly what was the same at her mom's house and dad's house. At both homes she had to take off her shoes before entering, brush her teeth at night, and not fight with her big brother. Jenny reported that she likes having her pets at her mom's house and being able to play outdoors there. At her dad's house, she likes having more movies to watch, and she likes that her dad plays board games with her. She is sad that the entire family doesn't play games together anymore.

Task 2. *Children gradually have to learn that it is not their job to take care of their parents.*

Strategy. Remind both parents and children that it is okay for the children to focus on their own world of school, friends, and outside activities. Some parents interpret a child's ability to set aside family problems as being selfish and noncaring. Remind parents that "children being children" is both healthy and necessary.

Encourage parents to continue their job of parenting. It's important that they focus time and energy on their children, provide consistent discipline, and set aside time for relaxation and fun in order to protect their children from long-term emotional problems.

Task 3. *Children must slowly process the loss of family.*

Strategy. Accepting the loss of family as Mom and Dad together is usually the single most difficult task for children. Children will often blame themselves for the divorce. This is safer than blaming one or both of the parents. Children younger than 10 usually don't know what they are feeling, how to put their feelings into words, or how to act out these feelings in behaviors that are not negative.

There are several effective counseling strategies that help children identify, verbalize, and finally confront and accept their feelings:

Use feeling cards or feeling charts to model and teach the words that express feelings. You can also use drawing, painting (especially finger paints), and dramatic play. As you teach the language of feelings, always give the message that all feelings are okay. Some feelings are dark, some are light, but they are all real, even if adults sometimes say, "Don't feel that way," or "You can't feel that way."

Have children draw their bodies (or have them lie down on top of newsprint paper and outline them). Then ask them to verbalize and color in what they feel where. For example, one child reported, "I get lumps in my throat when I say good-bye to my dad for a month," and another said, "My stomach feels on fire when Mom and Dad fight in front of me about paying child support."

Use puppets, dolls, or storytelling to allow children to talk indirectly about their feelings.

Use the Mutual Storytelling Techniques of Robert Gardner as a displacement strategy. Have the child create a "safe" story. Suggest a beginning for the story such as, Long, long ago in a faraway forest, there once lived a sad little animal named _____. When the child has finished telling the story, tell a similar story, using the same characters but offering hopeful, realistic solutions to the problems or puzzles happening in the child's story. Children like this strategy, especially if you record the story on tape (like a radio program) or on paper (make a book and ask the child to add illustrations). Gardner's book *Therapeutic Communication with Children* contains an excellent description of this counseling tool.

Reassure children that having positive feelings about the separation is not bad. Some children are relieved when divorce means a decrease in tension and fighting. Also, children may experience a pleasant increase in individual attention from each parent.

Task 4. *Children must learn that it is normal and okay to be angry at their parents for getting divorced.*

Strategy. This psychological task requires children to acknowledge and accept that parents are fallible. Often the custodial or primary parent becomes the main target for a child's anger because the child believes that this parent will not abandon him or her. It is too risky for a child to be angry with the absent, or visiting, parent. Part of the child's anger stems from the fact that no child would choose divorce as a solution to family difficulties. A child's classic question is, Why can't they stop fighting and be happy together? This seems like a logical solution to children.

Accomplishing this task partially depends on parents understanding and allowing the feelings of anger. The more vulnerable and insecure the parents are, the more difficulty they have allowing their children to be angry.

It is important for you, as the counselor, to validate the child's anger and to teach safe ways to express this anger. Anger is often scary to both the child and the parent. Remember to emphasize the rule of not hurting oneself, others, or property. Describe, model, and practice safe anger strategies with the child such as:

- throwing clay at a target
- throwing rocks in a pond, creek, or river
- smashing aluminum cans
- tearing paper
- hitting a mattress with an old tennis racket
- playing sports
- writing angry letters and tearing them up, and
- scribbling over and over on a page and then tearing or crumpling the page.

Task 5. *Children learn that divorce is not their fault and that it is not their job to make things better.*

Strategy. After children recognize, acknowledge, and express their anger, they can begin to let go of feeling responsible for the divorce. Girls are more likely than boys to side with the mother and to feel and to act responsible for her post-divorce difficulties. But both boys and girls may try to make things better by taking over adult tasks, such as cooking, cleaning, contributing money, or taking care of younger siblings.

Have the child make up a worry or fear list. Ask the child to identify which of these worries or fears are parent responsibilities and which are kid responsibilities. Follow up with a parent-child meeting in which the child can show the parent this list, talk about it, and decide who needs to "claim" or "fix" each worry or fear. Expect there to be worries that no one can fix.

Teach relaxation exercises. School-aged children respond well to creative visualization. Several helpful books are listed in the bibliography.

Task 6. *Children must learn that divorce means forever.*

Strategy. The task of accepting the permanence of the divorce requires children to resolve all of the previous tasks. This means that children must abandon any fantasies of reconciliation—a process that normally takes years. Parents are often surprised at how long these fantasies persist, often into a child's adulthood.

With children younger than eight, you can light a candle to mark the beginning of "private time." At the end of the session, the child blows out the candle and makes a wish. Talk about wishes, about what is real and what is fantasy. Over and over, children will wish for their parents to get back together. The counselor's job is to acknowledge the wish and then to talk about what is possible and what is not—to differentiate between fantasy, hopes, and reality.

Task 7. *Children need to accept their parents' divorce in order to allow themselves to love others and to be able to commit to and trust in the intimacy of an adult relationship.*

Strategy. This is an adolescent task. This final task of healing requires confronting and resolving old opinions, feelings, and unanswered questions about a divorce that may have happened months or years ago.

As a counselor, your central task is to help children understand and confront the crucial psychological tasks they must resolve. Your key work is to provide emotional support, to offer trust, privacy, and important information while remaining removed from family conflict and confusion.

What Parents Can Do

Counseling the child must include educating the parents. Guide parents to appropriate books and support groups and answer their questions about what they should do and say. This chapter includes a list of appropriate books for both parents and children. Encourage parents to read these books; in fact, give a weekly reading assignment. Also, encourage parents to select age-appropriate books for their child and to read them out loud with their child. A book can be a source of information as well as a tool for encouraging questions and sharing thoughts and feelings. The more parents understand how divorce affects a family, the better equipped they are to parent appropriately.

Encourage both parents to spend time with their children. Remind parents that they are their child's most important counselors. Emphasize two basic rules: First, parents should be honest. They should keep communications open and frequent. They can try to answer a child's questions simply and directly and also try to answer with information appropriate to the child's ability to understand. They don't have to worry about saying just the right words. What is said is not as important as simply taking the time to listen and to answer. Honesty minimizes fears and rebuilds security.

The second rule is to support the ex-spouse as a parent. Evaluate how much each parent emotionally supports the ex-spouse. Emphasize that every time a parent criticizes the other, the child is the one most hurt. Encourage parents to put aside their own needs and feelings, especially anger, and support the relationship between the child and the other parent. Long-term studies clearly show that it is hostilities between parents, rather than divorce, that harm children. Parental respect for each other and for each parent-child relationship minimizes conflicted loyalties for the children. Discuss steps toward forgiveness.

As part of educating parents, a few common myths need discussion. The first myth is that children are eager to talk about sad feelings. The opposite is more accurate. Children are reluctant to talk about painful feelings, especially if they sense that their words cause pain for their parents. If a mom's eyes begin to tear up, the child's reflex is to shut down. Children younger than 10 more naturally play or act out feelings, sometimes in positive ways, such as storytelling, drawings, and pretend play, but more often in negative ways, such as hitting other children, crying, or withdrawing.

The second myth is that children are aware of what they are feeling and that they understand the connection between feelings and behavior. Actually, it is difficult for most children to accurately label feelings, to explain in words what is bothering them—what is causing fear, sadness, or rage. Usually a child does not say, "I'm angry." Instead, he or she stomps around the house, slams the door, and yells at a younger sibling.

Myth number three is the expectation that children in emotional distress will act or appear sad and vulnerable, thus eliciting sympathy from adults. Often, this is not the case. Children who are upset are usually uncooperative and may even be obnoxious. These irritating behaviors will often trigger negative reactions from adults. The sadness and crying often occurs privately, especially if the child is of school age.

The fourth myth is that boys and girls react similarly to emotional trauma. In her long-term studies of children and divorce, Wallerstein observed that boys more quickly display noticeable signs of distress. Boys more often experience behavioral difficulties in school and conflicts with parents and peers. In contrast, girls present fewer observable symptoms in the first few years following divorce. However, Wallerstein noticed a "sleeper" phenomenon with many girls. As girls enter adolescence, they show conflicted feelings about serious dating and intimate relationships with men.

Repeatedly remind parents to continue to perform their essential tasks:

Task 1. *Parents must continue to be parents.*

Although they are experiencing their own sense of loss, confusion, and emotional crisis, their children cannot be temporarily set aside. Encourage and guide parents to get the support they need through groups, individual counseling, workshops, and books so that they can continue to function as effective parents.

Task 2. *Parents must learn about the impact of divorce on children.*

Encourage parents to learn all they can so that they can make good choices and be their children's guide in healing.

Task 3. *Divorced parents need to communicate directly with each other, not through their children.*

If parents cannot arrange visitation details or compromise on money issues, ask them to talk through a mediator, and stress that they must never talk through their children. Children should never be message carriers between warring adults and should never be asked to act as spies. Above all, children should not hear parents arguing about conflicts that have anything to do with them, such as money (who buys the new shoes), visitation, or household rules.

Task 4. *Parents need to understand that new relationships are a threat, not a delight, to children.*

Discuss with parents the importance of keeping dating separate from the family until a new relationship appears to be long-term. Accepting a new adult into the "family" generates a complex and usually painful mix of feelings for children. Loyalties are confused. The hope of reuniting Mom and Dad is threatened. If the relationship ends, the child experiences another loss.

Task 5. *Parents need to encourage their children to express feelings and to allow this expression without becoming offended, angry, or hurt, and without denying the children's right to their own feelings.*

Displacement is a communication technique that is helpful when discussing painful topics. If a child is asked directly, "How do you feel about your dad living with another woman?" the child will not want to answer directly. Instead, if the subject of the question is displaced (not "you" but some other person), the question becomes much safer. Ask, for example, What do you think about a dad who decides to move out and live with someone else? How do you think his kids feel? For younger children, the displaced subject can become an animal or the main character of a story or movie. For example ask, How did Cinderella feel when her father married such a mean new mom? Children of all ages are more open to talking about a safe "someone else" rather than their own situation.

What Teachers Can Do

Remind teachers not to assume that a child lives in a traditional two-parent family. In fact, according to the Annual Report of Household and Family

Characteristics (March 1994), only 55% of children in the United States live in a traditional nuclear family. Teachers should avoid making the nuclear family the "normal" family in classroom discussions and examples. Both fiction and nonfiction literature is now available that includes many types of family situations.

Encourage the child's parents to meet privately with the teacher and discuss the family situation. This is especially important during the first few years of separation and divorce. Support parents in seeking frequent communication with teachers to assess the impact of a divorce and/or visitation schedule on the child, academically as well as behaviorally and emotionally. Remind parents to notify a teacher of any significant changes (such as a modified visitation schedule) or events (such as a court hearing).

Remind teachers to find out which divorced parents can meet together at parent-teacher conferences, and which cannot. Also, it is important for a teacher to know which parent is responsible for assisting a child with homework and whether both parents should be sent school notices. It helps when teachers remember the "absent" parent and mail notices and school information directly to that parent.

Encourage teachers to report significant changes in school behavior to the custodial parent in a nonjudgmental manner. Parents may feel helpless or guilty about behavioral problems caused by divorce. Remind teachers and parents that school can be a safe place for many children, where they do not have to think about family problems but can enjoy being a kid.

COMMON ISSUES

The longer parents fight, the more traumatic divorce is for children. Conflicts between ex-spouses usually focus on child issues such as parenting, visitation, money, and power. These conflicts make a child feel even more responsible for causing the conflicts. As the therapist, do what you can to bring home the point that hostility hurts children. Remind parents that contested custody cases produce trauma and a great deal of stress, and that the longer the litigation, the slower the healing.

In cases where the parents are exceedingly hostile, suggest ways to minimize direct contact between the adults. Changing from one household to another is a tense situation for children under the best of circumstances.

Having one parent take the child to a neutral place, such as day care or school, where the other parent can then pick up the child, can reduce chances of conflict.

One parent may try to alienate the child from the other parent. The middle-school child is particularly likely to be judgmental of one parent's behavior. The child has probably learned to be very guarded and selective about what he or she says. Assessment of the child's relationship with either parent needs to be done indirectly with projective techniques.

For extreme situations, a guardian ad litem (G.A.L.) is court-appointed to represent the child in the legal system. It is crucial for the therapist to establish good communication with the G.A.L. in order to work together to promote the child's best interests. If you are working with a G.A.L., all recommendations, evaluations, or concerns should be in writing, with copies sent to all parties involved, especially the child's attorney. If possible, establish that as the child's therapist, you are working with and for the child and are responsible to the G.A.L., who is also the only person who can fire you. Establish who is responsible for fees and define the goals of therapy. Documentation of case management, phone contacts, and therapy notes are essential, since ongoing litigation is common. A licensed psychologist should supervise these cases.

DATING

When dating is casual, parents should keep the dating process separate from their children. Children's response to a parent dating will depend on their developmental age, the length of time since divorce, and the quality of parenting. In the year following the divorce, children need extra time and attention from both parents. The family is still processing the loss of the way things were and is still establishing new routines. Parents' time with their children should not be compromised or diluted by dating.

When dating occurs, encourage a parent to plan regular, dependable time with children without the dating partner. Common reactions expressed by children are jealousy, fear of losing a parent, conflicted loyalties, awkwardness about sexuality, and sadness about diminished chances of reconciliation. Both positive and negative feelings about the "new" adult are confusing. Children think, "If I like the woman Dad is dating, does that mean I like Mom less?" "If Dad kisses her, should I interfere?" "Would Mom feel hurt if I didn't ?" "If I don't like this woman, will I hurt Dad's feelings?"

ANTICIPATED PROGRESS AND OUTCOMES

Children whose parents divorce can grow up to be emotionally healthy adults. A child's adjustment depends on temperament, age, number of changes because of the divorce, and the degree of hostility between the parents. The most important factor is each parent's own adjustment; children will adjust to divorce about as well as their parents do. The quality of adjustment is important, for it will affect later long-term relationships.

Your work as a therapist involves helping the parents educate themselves about the effects of divorce on children, and helping the children express the strong emotions surrounding divorce. The combined goal is to facilitate an open, trusting relationship between parent and child. If parents listen to and communicate honestly with their children, they can help them work through the difficulties of most experiences, even divorce.

RESOURCES
Books for Parents, Teachers, and Counselors

Atlas, S. *The Parents without Partners Handbook*. Philadelphia, PA: Running Press, 1984.

For single parents. Practical tips for parenting.

Baris, M., and C. Garrity. *Children of Divorce: A Developmental Approach to Residence and Visitation*. Dekalb, IL: Psytec, 1988.

Describes children's emotional and behavioral responses to divorce at different developmental stages. For child and adolescent therapists.

_____. *Children Caught in the Middle*. New York, NY: Lexington Books, 1994.

Discusses the impact of a hostile divorce on children's development. An important resource.

Gardner, R. *Psychotherapeutic Approaches to the Resistant Child*. Garden City, NJ: Doubleday, 1977.

Filled with strategies to facilitate communication about painful topics. For counselors who work with children.

Kalter, N. *Growing Up Divorced*. New York, NY: Fawcett Columbine, 1990.

A practical book for parents. Suggests parenting strategies for different ages and describes different responses.

Klepsch, M., and L. Logie. *Children, Draw and Tell*. New York, NY: Brunner/Mazel, 1982.

For counselors. Describes how to use art as a projective technique to evaluate reactions to life events, such as divorce. Encourages communication.

Morgenbesser, M., and N. Nehl. *Joint Custody*. Chicago, IL: Nelson-Hall, 1994.

Covers joint custody, suggests questions to consider, and provides criteria to help determine whether the couple is acting appropriately.

Todd, K., and N. Barios. *Parenting Through Divorce*. Phoenix, AZ: Motiva Publishing, 1995.

A practical book written for the divorcing parents. It focuses on parenting issues and includes a helpful section on how to negotiate. Recommended for parents and counselors.

Wallerstein, J., and S. Blakeslee. *Second Chances: Men, Women and Children, A Decade After Divorce*. New York, NY: Ticknor and Fields, 1989.

An excellent summary of the research on children of divorce. May be too threatening for a parent in the early stages of divorce. For therapists.

Books for Children

Banks, A. *When Your Parents Get a Divorce: A Kid's Journal*. New York, NY: Puffin Books, 1990.

A workbook that encourages children to work through their thoughts and feelings.

Berger, T. *I Have Feelings.* New York, NY: Human Science Press, Inc., 1971.
Photographs of a boy expressing all of his feelings, including painful ones. Encourages identification of feelings.

Boulden, J., and J. Boulden. *Divorce and Remarriage Activity Book.* Santa Rosa, CA: Boulden Publishing Co., 1991.
Coloring book. Useful for identifying children's reactions.

Brown, L., and M. Brown. *Dinosaur's Divorce.* New York, NY: Little, Brown & Co., 1986.
Helps preschoolers discuss their parents' divorce.

Christiansen, C. *My Mother's House, My Father's House.* Atheneum, NY: Puffin Books, 1989.
Describes a school-aged girl's experience of living in two households. Beautifully written and illustrated.

Crary, E. *I'm Mad.* Seattle, WA: Parenting Press, 1992.
Helps children to explore safe, creative, even fun ways to express anger. Appropriate for children ages seven and younger.

Danziger, P. *The Divorce Express.* Boston, MA: G.K. Hall, 1988.
Written for children in middle school. A 15-year-old girl is resentful of her parent's divorce.

Gardner, R. *The Boys and Girls Book about Divorce.* New York, NY: Doubleday, 1977.
Will stimulate discussion about difficult topics. Includes several chapters for the older child.

Goff, B. *Where is Daddy?* Boston, MA: Beacon Press, 1969.

To be read by preschoolers and parents together. A powerful tool to help parents discuss the losses of divorce with their children.

Marcus, I., and P. Marcus. *Into the Great Forest: A Story for Children Away From Parents for the First Time.* New York, NY: Magination Press, 1992.

A delightful book for children, ages three to seven, who may have to leave one parent to visit another as a result of a separation or divorce. Written in a fairytale style.

Mayle, P., and A. Robin. *Why Are We Getting a Divorce?* New York, NY: Harmony Books, 1988.

For counselors or parents to read to children experiencing the divorce of their parents. Although humorous in the illustrations, the topics are powerful and should be read one chapter at a time. For children nine and younger.

Agencies and Organizations

KIDSRIGHTS
8902 Otis Avenue
Indianapolis, IN 46216

Catalog containing videos and books for children facing life's challenges.

Parents Without Partners
Publisher of Single Parent
8807 Colesville Rd.
Silver Spring, MD 20910
(301) 588-9354

CHAPTER 2

Stepfamilies and Blended Families

"Take out your paper and crayons," says the teacher. "Good. Now, please draw your family."

Rosa stares at the empty white paper, chews her pencil, squirms in her chair, and starts poking her classmate.

The teacher walks over. "What's wrong, Rosa? Why aren't you drawing?"

"Well," Rosa answers slowly, "I have two mothers and a new big brother. Where do I put everyone?"

Today, just as many children live in single, step, or blended families as in nuclear families. More than 60% of couples who remarry have children from a previous relationship. Stepfamilies are now a common family pattern, yet children in blended families report that they feel different, even abnormal. This is because programs offered by schools and other organizations are still designed to meet the needs of a nuclear family. Books, movies, commercials, and television have also been slow to reflect the change in family structure. The entertainment media still present the ideal family as the always-married couple with two or more biological children. No wonder Rosa struggles to draw her blended family.

Members of stepfamilies—parents and children—often believe that if they try hard enough, their new family will be a success, unlike their previous one. However, a stepfamily, created after divorce and remarriage, is different. The ghosts of past relationships affect the new relationships. Adults must create new solutions to family living and have only an unsuccessful model from which to work. It is crucial for parents, stepparents, children, and counselors to understand how stepfamilies are different from nuclear families.

STEPFAMILY DYNAMICS

A stepfamily is a family born from loss. (The word step is derived from the Old English word *stoep,* meaning "orphan" or "loss by death.") First there is the loss of the original family and the dreams that were part of it. Other losses may include homes, neighborhoods, friendships, and economic security.

There are several realities that affect the dynamics of every stepfamily. Both children and adults in the new family have previous histories, traditions, and rituals. Conflict is common when family members are asked to give up treasured celebrations, such as birthday parties or holiday rituals, because of visitation schedules.

The parent-child bond predates the couple bond. The newer and more vulnerable bond is the one between the couple. For most remarried couples, there is a lack of time to be alone with each other and strengthen the couple relationship.

There is usually another biological parent with power and influence over family members. For the children, this may mean more parental figures and loyalties to pull or confuse them.

Children are often members of two households. Behaviors, responsibilities, or attitudes that are accepted in one household may be unacceptable in the other, especially when religious beliefs or values are different.

Usually there is no legal relationship between stepparent and stepchildren. This means in practical terms that the stepparent cannot give permission for counseling or medical services without the biological parent's consent. More important, the permanence of the relationship between stepparent and child is not guaranteed or protected.

The Emotional Tasks of Stepchildren

The emotional tasks of children in a stepfamily include finding their place in the family and forming new relationships while grieving over the loss of their former family and continuing to experience the growth, change, and learning that take place during childhood. Specifically, here are a few of children's emotional and psychological challenges:

- *Unfinished mourning.* The remarriage is often the loss of the child's hope that Mom and Dad will get back together. The child may be angry at the new stepparent for destroying this dream.

- *Dealing with divided loyalty.* Children may entertain such thoughts as these: "Will I betray one parent by liking this new stepparent?" "If I begin to love this new adult, will I love my other parent less?" Even older children are confused and afraid that loving someone new means loving someone else less. These fears are increased if any of the adults fear being loved less. Also, children are often angry and scared because they are getting less attention from their newly married parent.

- *Questioning where they belong.* Children wonder, "Where is my real home? Can I belong to two homes?" The stress of moving between two households is difficult. The more changes there are (for example, in terms of siblings and stepsiblings, house rules, and living situations), the harder it is for children to adjust.

- *Confronting sexuality.* Suddenly a divorced parent is sharing a bed with another adult. Most children are uncomfortable realizing that their parents are sexual beings. Clear behavioral guidelines and boundaries for parents and children are critical, as are rules about privacy, nudity, affection, and sexual behavior.

- *Dealing with new siblings.* Children who suddenly have siblings, either part-time or full-time, have many dilemmas to resolve, such as ownership of bedroom and play space, toys, and even parents; changes in routines and discipline; and even "who bosses whom." If new stepsiblings change a child's birth order, the change is harder.

New Siblings

A significant challenge for children in a stepfamily is learning how to interact with new siblings. An excellent resource for adults is *Strangers in the House* by William Beer. Beer identifies five common sources of tension between stepsiblings:

1. *Equality of treatment by different parents.* Especially in the early years of a stepfamily, equal treatment of siblings from different families is not real-

istic or even reasonable. If a new stepmother attempts to treat her stepchildren the same as her biological children, feelings get hurt and tension increases. Another source of jealousy is when an "absent" parent (the visitation parent) showers gifts on his or her children, especially when the other children in the stepfamily receive nothing. There are no formulas for success, but the counselor can facilitate family discussion to identify sources of tension and resulting feelings.

2. *Competition for physical space.* This is the dilemma of "the invaders and the landlords." The more input children have about dividing up space, the more likely that tension and resentment will decrease. When space is limited, solutions need to be creative. Encourage parents to listen to the children's concerns and feelings and be sensitive to territorial issues.

3. *Change in birth order.* Acquiring new stepsiblings can change the birth order of a child in the new family. For example, an only child becomes the youngest because of two new older stepsiblings, or a first-born child gains two older stepbrothers and is no longer the "oldest." The greater the change in birth order, the harder the adjustment. Stepsiblings of the same gender and who are close in age face another problem. They want to be reassured that the parents realize how different they are rather than how alike. As a counselor, you may be able to help new siblings form alliances and thus decrease the fighting that often results when children attempt to reestablish the family pecking order. You can also help the family find ways for children to get the individual attention they seek from the biological parent.

4. *The birth of a child.* The birth of a child into a stepfamily seldom elicits joy and excitement in the stepsiblings. Instead, the stepsiblings often feel betrayed by the biological parents. A new baby is a sign that the stepfamily is permanent. The baby is also one more sibling with whom a child must compete for attention.

5. *Sexual boundaries.* New stepfamilies cannot assume that appropriate behavior will just happen between siblings who have no biological ties or history of growing up together. A counselor needs to help families establish clear guidelines for privacy. This is often a hard area for parents to talk

about with children. Rules about the bathroom are important, especially when families have limited space and several children. Help discussions remain specific and direct, such as *The bathroom door should be closed when someone's in the shower,* and *Don't enter anyone's room or the bathroom without knocking first.* Emphasize to parents that talking about sexuality and privacy decreases the risk of stepchildren crossing sexual boundaries.

ASSESSMENT

Behavioral Indicators

A child needs professional help when the following behavioral changes continue longer than a few months:

- withdrawal from family, peers, or school activities
- regression (for example, bedwetting, inability to sleep alone, toilet accidents during the day, excessive need of adult attention)
- aggression against other children or pets or destruction of favorite toys
- diminishing school performance
- increase in predelinquent behaviors, such as stealing at school or at home, coming home late, or experimenting with alcohol
- refusal to interact with stepsiblings or stepparent
- depression (see "Depression" chapter).

Assessment Tools

Projective techniques and incomplete sentences are two appropriate assessment tools for children who have difficulty with stepfamily issues. These tools are described in the "Divorce" chapter.

Key Issues to Explore

To understand the challenges that are specific to each stepfamily, the following information is important:

- How long ago was the original family dissolved by death, separation, or divorce?

- How new is the remarriage? How much time elapsed between the end of one family and the beginning of a new family? A live-in partner may have much of the same power as a stepparent.

- How often is the child part of another household? What is the visitation schedule? Do visits happen cooperatively or with tension?

- What is the relationship like between the ex-spouse and the new couple? Do the needs of the children come first?

- How long has the new couple been in a committed relationship? How strong is their bond? Do they save time and energy for each other? What issues are significant to them? How well are they finding solutions to these issues?

- What emotional tasks are the children confronting? Do the parents, step and biological, have empathy and understanding for the children's losses and changes? How does the child typically respond to stress?

- What changes have the children experienced during the past two years? Ask about such changes as a new school, new house, different bedroom, and new neighborhood. Evaluate what losses the children have experienced, such as family pets, friends, familiar room, even favorite toys. Has there been the birth of a baby?

- What development tasks will be appropriate for each child in the stepfamily?

Developmental Considerations

There are few written guidelines relating to the growth of the relationship between stepparent and child. A common error for a new stepparent is to assume a disciplinarian role before a trusting relationship is established. The child's reaction is anger, resentment, and rejection. This new adult is felt to be an intruder, someone challenging the child's loyalty to the biological parent.

Adults working with children in stepfamilies need to be aware that the development of relationships happens slowly and gradually. A parent's remarriage is a major life change for children, even when the remarriage is positive and accepted by all. At each developmental stage, children have age-appropriate ways of coping with the stress (or crisis) of becoming a stepchild. A counselor can help parents understand these different developmental responses.

Infants and toddlers adapt the most quickly to a remarriage. Most child psychologists recommend one primary home for young children so that a solid relationship is developed with the primary caretaker. Predictability and consistency should be encouraged; frequent change is stressful and disruptive.

Preschoolers respond to change by regressing. Regression appears behaviorally in the forms of bedwetting, temper tantrums, sleep difficulties, and/or an excessive demand for parental attention. At preschool, the child may also be more aggressive and demanding of attention. The peaceful cooperation of spouses and ex-spouses is needed to rebuild trust lost during separation and divorce. If needed, the therapist can help mediate agreements about child care, parenting routines, safety issues, visitation schedule adjustment, and discipline issues.

School-age children still hold onto magical thinking, hoping parents will reunite. When one parent remarries, this hope dies, and the child grieves even when the child loves the new parent. The child attracts parental attention by misbehaving. The underlying reasons for misbehavior often are:

- misdirected anger or sadness
- a cry for more attention, especially from the biological parent
- a loyalty conflict (children worry that loving a new parent means they are disloyal to the "old" parent)
- depression over the loss of hope that parents will reunite.

As children mature, they learn that they can love all the adults in their lives. However, before the child's love can expand to include the new parent, the child needs understanding, acceptance, and time in order to grieve over the loss of the original family. If misbehavior continues to escalate, counseling can provide the child with a safe, neutral place to express anger, grief, confusion, and frustration.

An additional issue for school-age children involves explaining their stepfamily to friends. Usually they don't. Being different is embarrassing; fitting in is a priority. Children at this stage often direct their anger about feeling different toward the primary custodial parent. Sometimes it is difficult for a mother to enforce consequences, particularly if her child mimics the aggressive behavior of an ex-spouse. In such a case, the goals of counseling are to teach safe ways of managing anger, identifying causes of the anger, and empowering the parent.

Adolescents have the most difficulty adjusting to a new stepfamily. Teens face a paradox. They are asked to enter a new family at a time when their developmental task is to become independent from their families. All teens need emotional distance to separate from family life, as well as time to be alone and to be with friends. Sexuality is a complicated, ever-present issue. Parental sexuality is a source of confusion, embarrassment, and even disgust. Also, conflict is normal at this age. The special counseling needs of teens are not covered in this handbook, but therapists must be aware of the difficult adjustment the teenager confronts.

INTERVENTION STRATEGIES

What Counselors Can Do

Adjusting to a step situation takes time, usually several years. Remind parents that the first year is usually the hardest. Encourage counseling. Explain that the many purposes of counseling include helping both parents and children understand the difficulties of making a new family; providing a safe, neutral place where difficult feelings can be expressed and clarified; and helping families develop strategies for resolving conflicts. Stepparents are expecting the type of joy that surrounds a first marriage. They are seldom prepared for the difficult and complicated emotional reactions of their children.

As the counselor, you first need to clarify the reasons for the referral. The most common concern is a child's misbehavior, either at home or at school. Because children may be very aware of what they are doing wrong, ask parents, with the child present, "What is the child doing right?" and "What are your child's strengths?" It is healing for a child to hear a parent talk about positive qualities. One question to ask the parent is, "If you woke up tomorrow and your child's problem was gone, how would your child behave differently?" (This is the miracle question from the Brief Therapy Model.)

The next task is to see the child alone and elicit the child's view of the stepfamily situation using interview and projective techniques.

Strategies for Dealing with Preschoolers. Four-year-old Dylan is hitting other children, talking only in baby talk, and throwing temper tantrums when his mother drops him off at day care. Dylan's biological father has moved out of state, and his mother has recently remarried.

Dylan's aggression and regression are red-flag behaviors. Through sand play and pretend play with puppets and a dollhouse, Dylan expressed fears, anger, and sadness about having less time with Mom and not seeing Dad. What should the counselor do?

1. Teach appropriate ways to express anger. These include dancing to wild music; scribbling and tearing paper; squishing and pounding clay; and running and jumping. Avoid using the "hit a pillow" technique because preschoolers generalize from pillows to playmates. Suggest that the parents read *I'm Mad* by Elizabeth Crary with their children.

2. Use displacement techniques (described in the "Divorce" chapter) to validate the child's anger and sadness over the multiple losses.

3. Encourage parents to discipline consistently and appropriately and to use nonphysical behavioral consequences such as time-out for aggressive behaviors. Also, remind parents to reinforce appropriate behaviors at home and at school with stickers, special treats, and quality one-on-one time.

4. Contact the "visitation parent" and suggest strategies for him or her to stay in touch with a young child. *Children of Divorce* by Baris and Garrity has an excellent chapter on long-distance parenting.

5. Encourage the primary parent to schedule more one-on-one time with the child. Educate parents, teachers, and other involved adults about the dynamics of unfinished mourning for the loss of the original family.

6. Encourage the biological parent to be the disciplinarian whenever possible. During the first year of a new marriage, the stepparent needs to play

with and simply be with the child.

The goal of solution-focused treatment is to strengthen child-parent relationships. In Dylan's case, the mother called the biological father and requested frequent, routine communication with Dylan (calling days were marked on the calendar). Mother and father worked together, and after a few weeks Dylan's aggressive behaviors decreased. At this age, the counseling focus is on the parents and how they can modify their parenting to meet the child's needs.

Strategies for Dealing with Older Children. Eight-year-old Caitlin is in trouble at school for daydreaming, not finishing her work, and failing subjects in which she usually does well. Two years ago, her parents divorced, and she and her mother moved to a nearby town. Recently, her father married a woman whom Caitlin likes. But since the marriage, Caitlin refuses to do anything her stepmother asks and quarrels with her about everything.

During the elementary school years, children are usually referred to counseling because of misbehavior at school or a sudden slip in grades. Typical misbehaviors are:

• aggressive behavior toward peers or teachers

• poor grades, changes in academic performance/attitude

• attention-seeking behaviors

• excessive daydreaming or irritability.

The clue for the counselor is that the symptoms are timed with stepfamily issues, such as remarriage of a parent, new siblings, a change in a parent's visitation schedules, birth of a sibling, or a parent moving away. The target of sadness and anger is the new marriage partner, the stepparent. Here are some strategies for the counselor:

• Use Gardner's Mutual Storytelling Technique described in the "Divorce" chapter and read *Double Dip Feelings* by Barbara Cain. This book validates children having two contrasting feelings at the same time. Children in stepfamilies often experience conflicting, uncomfortable, and confusing feelings. For example, children hate that their parents are divorced, but they still love them. Encourage parents to read this book with their children.

- Suggest regular family meetings. Have parents and children establish house rules together. Encourage new stepparents to back away from the discipline role.

- Educate the stepparent and parents on the mourning process for children, and explain how misbehavior is a symptom and "cover-up" for grieving.

- Identify ways children can have power, influence, and attention in a family other than by misbehaving.

- Tell parents that current research on stepfamilies strongly suggests that in the best of situations, it takes two to four years for a new family to adjust to living together.

- Be prepared to meet with various subgroups within the child's family, including the remarried couple, biological parents, stepparent, and other children.

- Teach life skills such as stress management, use of words to express feelings, conflict resolution techniques, anger management, and parenting skills. Stepparents often find themselves suddenly parenting children of ages with which they have had little experience.

- Encourage children 10 years and older to use a journal. Suggest recording highs and lows of the week, topics they want to discuss in counseling, and incidents about which they want to let off steam. *Creative Journaling for Children* by Capacchione has wonderful ideas to facilitate expression. Use the journal to look back, mark progress, and set goals. Encourage older children to read both fiction and nonfiction books about divorce and stepliving. Identifying with a character in a novel is a healing way of realizing that others feel similar conflicting feelings.

- Refer the child to the school counselor for life-changing groups. Children benefit from knowing that they are not alone in their feelings and reactions.

What Parents Can Do

As a counselor, emphasize patience. Anger from impatience is a key problem. The adults are tired of conflict and change and want their new family to settle into a pleasant, positive routine. They want the children to be happy about this new marriage but often feel angry, frustrated, and overwhelmed with the children's negativity as well as the many stresses of a new marriage. They may feel short of time, energy, space, and money. The new couple often wishes the ex-spouses were "out of the picture" so that old issues weren't constantly stirred up. Sometimes they wish the children were out of the picture, too, so that they could be newlyweds in a first marriage. It is important for parents to do the following:

- Schedule regular time for themselves. If this new couple bond fails, the family fails. The couple should engage in short-term counseling if any of the following are unresolved: financial and living-space arrangements; or parenting roles, styles, rules, or issues from the previous marriage.

- Allow time for biological parents to be with their children.

- Lower their expectations. The goal of a perfect family with well-behaved children in a calm, harmonious, neat home is unrealistic.

- Schedule regular family meetings. Meetings must be kept positive and allow enough time for everyone to have the chance to air complaints and make requests. As a counselor, you can help to model a meeting during a family session. Families can use their meeting time to plan fun activities, to reinforce what is going well, to identify problems, and to make and renegotiate house rules. (If a large age difference exists between stepsiblings, sometimes the younger siblings could have an alternative activity at meeting time.)

- Learn more about stepfamilies. Books, schools, continuing education centers, mental health centers, and counselors are all possible sources of information. Seek support when family stresses intensify. Talk to other stepparents and, if possible, join a step support group or attend parenting classes.

- Schedule time for relaxation. This is crucial because the many family changes, needs, and conflicts are stress-producing.

- Go slowly in showing physical affection. Early in the stepparent-stepchild relationship, use words instead of hugs. Remind parents that the older the children, the longer it takes them to accept a stepparent.

What Teachers Can Do

The classroom teacher can no longer make assumptions about the family situation within which a student lives. Early in the school year, teachers should identify for each student:

- what adults are important to the student
- if the child is involved in a visitation schedule, and if so, what it is
- who does the day-to-day parenting
- who helps with schoolwork
- what life changes the student has experienced.

Encourage teachers to include, if possible, all interested adults in the parent-teacher conference or have reports sent to them. Teachers should talk to the child and ask who should be included. Remind teachers to try to remain neutral and nonjudgmental. If a parent lives in a distant location, a teacher can ask whether the parent should be added to the school's mailing list.`

Remember, children younger than 10 usually convert intense feelings into negative behavior. Encourage teachers, then, to listen to what children are telling them through their behavior and to validate feelings without trying to fix the situation. Teachers should remind children that they cannot fix adult problems and that their work is to learn at school. School can provide children with many opportunities to achieve mastery and to focus on what they *can* do. This may be encouraging to the child who cannot do anything about changes at home.

COMMON ISSUES

When the divorced parents cannot co-parent cooperatively, trouble and stress are inevitable. Everyone continues to be caught in the parental conflict and the unresolved divorce. Ask parents to meet with a professional mediator, especially if the divorce was hostile, if remarriage has triggered resentment, if visitation schedules are being argued, or if legal battles continue to be waged.

One of the most common mistakes stepparents make is having unrealistic expectations about the behavior or feelings of the children, such as expecting their children to automatically love the new spouse, or expecting stepchildren to call them "Mom" or "Dad." The more rigid and defensive a parent is about how family members should feel or act, the more likely that parent will be disappointed and angry.

The most problematic relationship is often between stepmother and stepdaughter. If the daughter is an adolescent, turmoil and conflict can be expected. The child is at a developmental stage when she would be pushing away from any mother figure and wanting the attention and approval of her father. Encourage stepmothers to back away and focus on behavior rather than feelings or attitudes. *The Good Stepmother: A Practical Guide* by Savage and Adams is a valuable resource for all stepmothers.

Another common problem occurs when one family is willing to modify its parenting, but the other family is not—for example, when one set of parents sets all the limits and does all of the disciplining. This is an extremely frustrating situation and does make parenting difficult—but not impossible. Children can learn to behave as expected in different situations, so long as hostility can be minimized.

ANTICIPATED PROGRESS AND OUTCOMES

Since the trigger for referral is usually misbehavior, aggressive or regressive, the signs of success are a decrease in misbehavior and an increase in positive behavior. Ask parents to assess improvement by answering these questions:

- How does your child respond to stress or intense feelings now?

- Is your child able to do things other than hit, yell, or otherwise show aggression when he or she is upset?

- Has your child returned to a child's world and have stepfamily issues faded into the background?

- Have regressed behaviors, such as baby talk and sleeping with a parent, decreased?

- Can your child use words to express thoughts, feelings, and frustrations?

- Have parents been able to compromise on parenting differences?

- In school, has your child been able to focus more on schoolwork and worry less about family problems?

- Is your child playing with friends more appropriately?

- Are conflicts less frequent between family members?

Questions like these help parents see progress. During stressful days, it may be difficult to recognize progress, and it may be hard to remember that building a stepfamily takes time and energy. Remind parents of these six characteristics of an integrated stepfamily identified by Visher and Visher (1989):

1. Family members have mourned and accepted their losses.

2. Stepparents have realistic expectations for themselves and their children.

3. The couple bond has remained strong, loving, and unified.

4. The stepfamily has created its own positive family rituals.

5. Step relationships are satisfactory.

6. All parent figures can usually cooperate for the benefit of the children.

The building of a stepfamily is not a linear process. Usually there is some progress, followed by change. Change is stressful. Often when change occurs, everything may seem to "fall apart again" before more progress is seen. This process happens in any kind of family, but it is sometimes particularly hard for stepfamilies to keep this in mind. However, if the bond between the parents remains positive and continues to grow, the dynamics within a stepfamily will continue to improve.

RESOURCES

Books for Parents, Teachers, and Counselors

Allan, J. *Inscapes of the Child's World.* Dallas, TX: Spring Publications, 1988.

Teaches how to use art and sand tray as healing tools. Included is a comprehensive description of the "rosebush" exercise.

Beer, W. *Strangers in the House.* New Brunswick, NJ: Transaction Books, 1989.

Excellent resource for understanding and improving stepsibling relationships.

Bloomfield, H. *Making Peace in Your Stepfamily*. New York, NY: Hyperion, 1993.

Includes many exercises to practice with a family who may feel overwhelmed with stepfamily issues.

Cappachione, L. *Creative Journaling for Children*. Boston, MA: Shambhala Publishing, 1989.

Useful for counselors and teachers to encourage the process of writing to work through feelings.

Faber, A., and E. Mazlish. *How to Talk So Kids Will Listen and Listen So Kids Will Talk*. New York, NY: Avon Books, 1980.

Practical strategies for new stepparents and for biological parents.

Kashet, J. *Love and Power in the Stepfamily: A Practical Guide*. New York, NY: McGraw-Hill, 1986.

Overview of the dynamics of stepfamilies.

Klepsch, M., and L. Logie. *Children Draw and Tell*. New York, NY: Brunner/Mazel, 1982.

A valuable resource for counselors. Its focus is on drawing as a projective technique to evaluate and encourage communication about self and family.

Newman, M. *Stepfamily Realities*. Oakland, CA: New Harbinger Press, 1994.

Written by a stepparent who is also a therapist. Provides parenting advice and suggestions for self-care for the adults in the family.

Savage, K., and P. Adams. *The Good Stepmother: A Practical Guide*. Knob Noster, MO: Crown Publishers, 1988.

Describes the realistic challenges of stepparenting. A reassuring book for the stepmother and biological parent.

Visher, E., and J. Visher. *How to Win as a Stepfamily* (2nd ed.) New York, NY: Brunner/Mazel, 1992.

Second edition of a classic; lots of practical advice.

Books for Children

Berman, C. *What Am I Doing in a Stepfamily?* Secaucus, NJ: Carol Publishing, 1992.

A picture book that is useful for a variety of ages. The humorous illustrations will encourage discussion about stepfamily changes.

Berry, J. *Good Answers To Tough Questions: About Stepfamilies.* Chicago, IL: Childrens Press, 1992.

Gives practical suggestions for children in a new blended family.

Cain, B. *Double Dip Feelings.* New York, NY: Magination Press, 1990.

Practical picture book for children under seven to invite discussion about having conflicting feelings.

Cook, J. *Room for a StepDaddy.* Morton Grove, IL: Albert Whitman & Co., 1995.

Joey has trouble accepting his new stepfather, but with the constant love of all the parents, he learns that there is love enough for all.

Crary, E. *I'm Mad.* Seattle, WA: Parenting Press, 1992.
Teaches safe, creative ways to express anger. For children ages seven and younger.

Getzoff, A., and C. McClenahan. *Stepkids: A Survival Guide for Teenagers in Stepfamilies.* New York, NY: Walker, 1984.

Appropriate for middle school children. Normalizes common reactions to a changing family and offers advice on how to cope with a new family.

Agencies and Organizations

Stepfamily Association of America
650 J Street, Suite 205
Lincoln, NE 68508
(800) 735-0329

Publishes a stepfamily bulletin full of useful and professionally formulated advice.

National Council on Family Relations
3989 Central Ave., Suite 550
Minneapolis, MN 55421
888-781-9331

Stepfamily Foundation
333 West End Ave.
New York, NY 10023
(212) 877-3244

CHAPTER 3

Grieving

Jenny's Aunt Sue knocked at the classroom door, spoke quietly to the teacher, then motioned for Jenny to leave. School wasn't out for another two hours. Jenny's stomach knotted. Had she done something wrong?

Together, they went to Aunt Sue's house. It was quiet, empty. Jenny could hear the clock ticking. It was never that quiet at her own house. Her little sister, Jessica, was always following her around—talking, interrupting, asking a million questions. What a pest! Where was Jessica anyway? And where were her mom and dad? Why wouldn't her aunt answer her questions?

The phone rang. Her aunt answered it and started crying. Jenny had never seen her aunt cry before. Jenny wanted her mom and dad *now*. When they finally arrived, they hugged her too tight and felt far, far away. Her mom was crying, and her dad began to explain that her sister, Jessica, was gone.

Jenny didn't understand. "Gone where?" Jenny asked. "When is she coming back?"

When a child experiences the death of a parent or a sibling, everything changes. The loss affects his or her life at home and school, as well as relationships with family and friends. The remaining parent—or both parents if it was a child who died—feels distant or different, even unapproachable; parents in acute mourning are often lost in their own grief and are unaware of their children's needs. Family routine is lost, and this often means that school and after-school activities are neglected. Friendships often change. Other children may distance themselves if the child's mood swings alternate from indifferent or withdrawn to angry or obnoxious. Perhaps the most important change is that the child's belief in a safe and predictable world is lost. A child may suddenly be afraid to leave home, even to go to school.

Every year in the United States, nearly two million children younger than 15 experience the death of a sibling or parent. This trauma can cause acute as well as chronic emotional and behavioral symptoms. For example, 90% of children in chemical-dependency programs have lost a parent. Counseling can prevent some of these long-term disturbances.

ASSESSMENT

When assessing to what degree the child is affected by his or her grief, there are some specific criteria to look for:

- *How well is the family coping?* A child's ability to grieve mirrors the family's ability to grieve. Interview the child's primary caretaker. To what degree has the family's daily routine returned to normal? Is the loss talked about at home? Is it okay for adults and/or children to express their emotions? Is it all right to cry?

- *In what stage of grief is the child?* Children go through the same grief stages as adults, but not necessarily in the same order. Particularly with sudden loss, children can move from anger to denial, to bargaining, to sadness, to acceptance—in any order. They also react to the emotional climate of their family. If the family gets stuck at any one stage, most likely the child will get stuck there, too.

- *In what stage of grief are the parents?* The longer that a child feels the emotional distance of his or her parents, the greater the child's trauma.

- *How long has the child felt alone or afraid?* Have the parents reconnected with the child? Gently point out how emotional closeness is avoided when a parent is tired, irritable, or lost in the crush of a frantic work schedule. Work can become a place of escape for a grieving parent.

- *How long ago did the loss occur?* Grieving increases during the anniversary time of the death, especially the first-year anniversary. Subsequent losses—even smaller ones, such as the death of a pet or saying good-bye to a special teacher or to a friend who is moving away—can trigger old feelings.

• *Has normal grieving become clinical depression?* A sad child needs to spend time and energy thinking about and feeling the loss. After a few weeks, most children are able to resume activities at school and with friends; they then grieve when they are alone, usually at home.

Diagnostic Criteria

Typical emotional-behavioral disruptions include:

• more time spent daydreaming

• difficulty concentrating on schoolwork

• difficulty remembering assignments and chores

• a short time of withdrawal (one to two months) from the usual activities, sports, and hobbies; temporary school phobia

• difficulty sleeping and fear of being alone

• modest and temporary increases in negative and aggressive behavior—verbal or physical—with friends or family members.

Abnormal emotional-behavorial disruptions that indicate clinical depression include:

• chronic school problems such as poor attendance, behavior problems, or failing grades

• normal disruptions that last longer than a few months

• negative, tumultuous interactions with family or friends that result in a high incidence of accidents, fights, or injuries

• suicidal thinking or planning.

Assessment Tools

The most effective assessment tools to use with children and adolescents who are grieving are the Reynolds Child Depression Scale and the Reynolds Adolescent Depression Scale.

Every child responds differently to stress. For example, some children become too quiet, others "too good," and others too negative. The type of behavioral change does not reflect the degree of disturbance. For instance, angry outbursts are no more or less serious than sad tears. An accurate assessment of the degree of disturbance is based on two criteria. The first criterion is the extent of behavioral change. How much change has taken place and in how many different environments? For example, has the child become aggressive at home and at school, or only at home? Within a few weeks, most children begin to behave more like themselves at school; it generally takes longer for children's behavior to return to normal at home.

Predicting the Degree of Trauma to the Child

The loss of a parent is the greatest trauma. Few experiences make life feel as unsafe and unpredictable as the abrupt loss of a parent. An unexpected, sudden loss is more traumatic than an anticipated loss.

The death of a sibling, relative, or family friend affects the entire family. A child then has to cope with his or her own feelings and the feelings of parents and sometimes with the emotional loss of parents, as they become distant in their grief.

The more parents cast blame for the loss, the more likely a child will feel responsible for not preventing the death. For example, a child may think, *I was sick, too, but why didn't I die?* Even young children can feel guilty following a death. It is a natural human response to feel as if a death or trauma could have been prevented. Children and adults may think that if they had done something differently, they could have prevented the tragedy.

The more changes in a child's routine, the more stress a child feels. It is important, then, to inquire into any changes that have taken place as a result of the death. Has there been a change of residence? Has the child changed schools? Has he or she lost friends?

Medical expenses place additional stress on a family and could mean that a parent has to work longer hours or take on an extra job, and that the child is left in childcare or at home alone.

The emotional recovery of the parents is the most critical factor in predicting the emotional recovery of the child.

Developmental Considerations

Children younger than five seldom understand that death is final. As children grow, their understanding of the finality of death increases, and their sadness changes. They continue to grieve throughout childhood—not all the time, but certainly at times of significant events such as starting first grade, beginning to menstruate, or graduating from high school.

Children in grade school have the additional resources of peers and teachers. A best friend, supportive teammates, understanding teachers and coaches—these are all people who can listen, empathize, and encourage. They also offer normal routine and healthy "time-outs" from being sad. Children who isolate themselves from friends increase their risk of becoming significantly depressed.

As children mature, they reprocess earlier traumas at deeper levels of understanding and sometimes at deeper levels of pain. Adolescents in particular may re-experience their loss and grief with adult understanding and feeling.

INTERVENTION STRATEGIES
What Counselors Can Do

Here are some useful cognitive strategies:

- *Explore issues around guilt.* To what degree does the child comprehend how and why the death or loss occurred? Ask the child to explain to you what happened and listen for feelings of guilt and responsibility. Younger children, especially those younger than five, have fantasies about what they can do to turn death around. Older children may become immersed in taking care of their siblings or parents. Help children understand that it is not their job to make things better or to make adults feel better. Give the child permission to be alive and to feel happy without feeling guilty. Help the child to feel okay about playing and having fun after someone, especially a sibling, has died.

- *Provide information.* Allow children to ask the morbid questions that they may have been afraid or too embarrassed to ask. They may want to know very specific information about what happens to the body after death: Does it really get stiff? Can worms or bugs get into the casket? Do fingernails keep growing?

• *Enable the child to express his or her feelings.* Provide a safe place for the child to mourn, to replay the trauma, or to change the ending through play therapy. (Let the child be the guide in choosing the form of play—dolls, creative storytelling, drawings, or sand tray.) Allow the child to work through a feeling or theme over and over again. The experience of loss has many parts to it. Following are some of the goals during play therapy:

1. *Help the child achieve mastery through repetition.* Adults talk and retell to help themselves heal from trauma. Children play, replay, and reenact to heal. Your role as therapist is to listen, to clarify, to interpret, and to support. Sometimes the support means holding and hugging. Listen and watch without criticizing, crying, or withdrawing. This approach allows the child to ask questions as well as to act out feelings in a safe, accepting place. The child can work it out—replay or retell the trauma—until feelings are resolved. This takes time.

2. *Assess the child's level of understanding.* The therapist can gently correct misunderstandings, using more accurate terms (such as "dead," not "went away" or "sleeping" or "gone"), and can address the child's egocentric thoughts (no, the child did not cause the disaster to happen and couldn't have prevented it).

3. *Encourage the child to ask for what he or she needs.* Directly with words, or indirectly through play, pictures, and stories, children will ask for what they need. Sometimes you will need to provide interpretation when the child doesn't understand what is being asked. Often children need comfort and reassurance. They may want to talk about new fears, such as fear of the dark or fear of someone else dying. They may ask you to help them find a way to say good-bye to the person who died, such as writing a letter or making a picture or a gift. It is not unusual for children to need permission and help in expressing, *I'm angry; why did you die and leave me?*

4. *Help the child label feelings.* While a child is working out thoughts and feelings during play therapy, you can help give a label to the feeling and provide acceptance. Talk about how important it is to express feelings.

Children may also somatize; stomachaches may mean, "I'm afraid." Discuss how feelings affect behavior, causing both positive and negative actions. Belligerent behavior can be an expression of sadness or anger; sometimes when children feel sad, they ask for a hug, but sometimes they tease their sister. Adults, too, are sometimes unable to express their feelings and needs directly. Explain to both the child and the parents that it is difficult to understand how a person is feeling simply by watching how he or she behaves.

Some behavioral strategies that have proved effective are journal writing or drawing; teaching safe anger behaviors (for examples, see "Divorce" chapter); and relaxation and creative visualization methods using themes of safety, security, and peaceful relaxation (appropriate visualizations include magic carpet, guardian angel, magic wish, or secret clubhouse).

What Parents Can Do

Remind parents that grieving takes time. Individuals grieve in their own way and at their own pace.

Support the choice to seek counseling. Reassure a parent that it is a sign of strength, not weakness, to seek help from clergy, friends, or counselors. It is normal and healthy for a child to need a friend or counselor outside the family, who will listen and console. Encourage parents to reach out to their own support networks for emotional help. Mourning is difficult and lonely. Often family members are lost in their own grief and simply cannot give the emotional support to others in the family.

Talk about the loss and remind parents and children that it is okay to cry. Sharing sorrow is a healthy way to get through the grief and helps people go on. Suggest having a regular time to talk, but at a time when the child is willing. Be sure that parents understand that there is a difference between grieving and dwelling on the loss. Let the child guide how much talking is needed. Preschool children often ask the same questions over and over. School-age children are eager to get back to school and friends.

Encourage listening. Explain how it is different from rescuing or problem solving. Emphasize that a child has a right to his or her own feelings. The adult simply needs to listen and acknowledge that the child's feelings are real and are important enough to say out loud. Model active listening during a counseling session with a parent and child. Discuss discipline. It is appropriate for the usual rules and expectations to be relaxed, but maintaining positive discipline and behavioral limits is essential. Children are reassured that their family will be okay when parents notice misbehavior and correct it. Children become anxious and insecure when misbehavior escalates and parents do nothing. Adolescents especially need positive but firm limits and discipline.

During times of family stress, children need additional love, support, and structure. The younger the child, the more likely behavior will regress. For example, a child might suddenly be afraid to sleep alone or to be left at day care. As the family heals, these immature behaviors will diminish. Reassure parents that it is healthy for a school-age child to seek other situations where life is normal—with friends, at school, and with neighbors—where he or she can temporarily step away from grieving.

What Teachers Can Do

Be sure the child's teacher knows about the loss. Speak with the teacher, at least by phone, to evaluate how the child is coping at school. Encourage the teacher to allow for some behavioral regression, aggressive acting out, daydreaming, or withdrawing.

Suggest that the teacher offer emotional support and attention. Usually, older children will not want to be singled out or treated differently from their peers. Private times to talk with the student before or after school or during recess could be offered.

Ask the teacher to contact the parent, school counselor, or you if the child shows extreme or chronic changes in behavior or signs of chronic depression. Explore with the teacher support systems for the child at school, such as group counseling or peer counseling. Many schools now offer life-changing groups.

COMMON ISSUES

Grieving is a developmental process that continues as children mature. As they grow, children ask new questions and ask the old ones again. For example, if a sibling died of cancer, an older child may want to know specific information about the illness. Feelings of sadness and loss deepen as a child begins to understand the finality of death and the meaning of forever.

Post-traumatic Stress Disorder symptoms are triggered by new changes. If a loss was sudden and the child was present and involved, such as in a car accident, a child may become hypervigilant and hyperresponsive. An increased startle response may last several years. Review the symptoms and treatment of Post-traumatic Stress Disorder described in the "Traumatized Children" chapter.

A child feels guilt when a sibling dies, perhaps remembering specific times the surviving child was mean, acted out, or refused a request. If a long illness preceded the death, the child may have had normal but negative feelings of resentment, anger, and jealousy during the illness, and may have even wished the sick sibling would die so that life could be normal again. A child will be ashamed of those feelings, especially after the sibling does die. Help the child talk out these feelings and be reassuring that all the different feelings are normal. Play therapy, writing, drawing, talking through puppets—all of these can facilitate expression.

The younger the child, the more likely egocentric thinking will increase guilt. The child may entertain ideas such as: *Did my thoughts cause the death? Why didn't I die?* A young child, but even an adolescent, will also wonder what they can do to "fix" things.

Besides the sadness, anger, and guilt, children also feel fear. They may worry. *Who will die next? Is death contagious?* Children often develop new fears, especially about the safety of everyone they love, and don't want to be separated from family members. Maintaining close physical proximity is one way to keep someone safe. Refusing to go to school is often a child's attempt to keep the family safe.

Grieving is individual. Expressions of grief vary from the extremes of denial—showing no emotion—to negative and angry behavior. Help the parent recognize the child's usual response to stress. This behavioral pattern will be the best predictor of future responses to stress and a reliable guide to interpreting the child's feelings and degree of emotional-behavioral disturbance.

Generally, boys react with aggressive behavior. They will argue, hit, fight, and verbally strike out. They may tease playmates, pick fights with their friends, or, more passively, refuse to do schoolwork. Meanwhile, they might say that they don't feel sad or miss the person who died. Usually, boys will tend to push adults away.

Girls, on the other hand, often tend to seek out comfort from adults. Girls are more likely than boys to regress, withdraw, or become weepy. A girl may show sadness by seeking physical closeness, asking to be held, especially at night, or by asking to sleep with a parent. Girls are more likely to ask directly for what they need. Remember, however, that some boys will react with sadness that is apparent, and that some girls may react with aggression.

ANTICIPATED PROGRESS AND OUTCOMES

If a child is in counseling because of a parent's request, then the parent is aware of the child's distress. This awareness will help the child recover. During the year following a death or loss in a family, children should gradually resume their usual interests and activities. Their behavior and routines—eating, sleeping, school, and activity patterns—should return to normal. They should look and act like the kids they were by behaving in ways that are not too good and not too bad. After a year's time, if a child's behavior or affect is still significantly altered, the child needs help. At this point, let us hope that the family will recognize that professional counseling is appropriate. Remember that counseling a child through grieving means assisting the family through grieving.

Anniversary times trigger strong feelings. One year after a death is often a difficult time for the family. Strong emotions resurface. Parents may become depressed, irritable, or unapproachable, but may ignore the reason for these feelings and may never verbally acknowledge the anniversary. Children sense their parents' emotional state and feel their distance; this can confuse them and make them afraid that once again their world is falling apart. Families may find it helpful to share grieving by planning an "anniversary celebration" where the family comes together to speak about the one who died, to mourn together, and to celebrate the sharing of life and death. If a parent can reassure a child that as time passes, pain diminishes, the child will also be helped in reaching that final stage of grieving—acceptance.

RESOURCES
Books for Parents, Teachers, and Counselors

Fitzgerald, H. *The Grieving Child: A Parent's Guide.* New York, NY: Simon & Schuster, 1992.

Covers the basics of how children grieve and gives suggestions on how to encourage healing.

Furman, E. *A Child's Parent Dies.* New York, NY: Yale University Press, 1974.

Helps adults understand the impact of a parent's death on a child.

Grollman, E. *Talking About Death: A Dialogue Between Parent and Child.* Boston, MA: Beacon Press, 1976.

A read-along picture book designed to encourage a dialog about death. Includes explanations and resources parents may find valuable.

Kroen, W. *Helping Children Cope With the Loss of a Loved One: A Guide for Grownups.* Minneapolis, MN: Free Spirit Press, 1996.

Clear and concise information on how children perceive and react to death, and offers support strategies.

Kubler-Ross, E. *Death, the Final Stage of Growth.* New York, NY: Prentice Hall, 1975.

One of the first books written about death and dying and the human response. Kubler-Ross was a pioneer in describing the stages a person goes through in response to a loved one dying.

Books for Children

Clifton, L. *Everett Anderson's Good-bye.* Holmes, PA: The Trumpet Book Club, Reading Rainbow Book, 1983.

A picture book suitable for the child younger than seven. This is a touching story about a young boy sorting out his feelings after the death of his father.

Countant, H. *First Snow.* New York, NY: Knopf Publishers, 1974.

Fiction. With the help of her grandfather, a little Vietnamese girl begins to understand how death can be accepted as a natural part of life.

dePaola, T. *Nana Upstairs, Nana Downstairs.* New York, NY: Putnam, 1973.

Fiction. Picture book for young children that tells the story of a boy's love for his grandparents and his acceptance of their deaths.

Krementz, J. *How It Feels When a Parent Dies.* New York, NY: Knopf, 1981.

Nonfiction. True stories from children about their reactions to their parents' death. For the school-age child.

LeShan, E. *Learning To Say Good-Bye When a Parent Dies.* New York, NY: Macmillan, 1976.

Nonfiction. Discusses the fears, fantasies, and questions that children experience when a parent dies.

Mellonie, B., and R. Ingped. *Lifetimes.* New York, NY: Bantam, 1983.

A small picture book for children younger than six which explains the concept of death in a straightforward manner.

Paterson, K. *Bridge to Terabitha.* New York, NY: Harper Collins, 1977.

Newberry Award-winning fiction for middle school ages. A 10-year-old boy befriends a newcomer, who then unexpectedly dies.

Rylant, C. *Missing May.* New York, NY: Orchard Books, 1992.

Fiction. 1993 Newberry Award winner. After the death of her beloved aunt who raised her, 12-year-old Summer searches for reasons to go on. Ages 10 and younger.

Spinelli, J. *Maniac Magee.* New York, NY: Scholastic, 1991.

Fiction for middle school child. Newberry Award winner. Story of a young boy, orphaned at age three, who uses his athletics and friendship in a magical way to bring unity to other children. Humorous and thoughtful.

Steiner, B. *Brother Whale.* New York, NY: Walker, 1988.

A beautiful picture book for the younger child; an Alaskan boy learns about death from a dying whale.

Viorst, J. *The Tenth Good Thing About Barney.* New York, NY: Atheneum, 1979.

Fiction. A wonderful book for the younger child which addresses how to say good-bye to a loved one.

Agencies and Organizations

Centering Corporation
P. O. Box 337
Omaha, NE 68103

This organization provides supportive literature to grieving children and their families.

Bereaved Children's Program
Westchester Jewish Community Services
141 North Central Avenue
Hartsdale, NY 10530

The Dougy Center
P. O. Box 86852
Portland, OR 97286

The Compassionate Friends
P. O. Box 1347
Oak Brook, IL 60521

Hope for the Bereaved
1342 Lancaster Avenue
Syracuse, NY 13210

CHAPTER 4

Attention Deficit/Hyperactivity Disorder

Maria's brother was diagnosed with ADHD at age 12. He tinkered continually. He tore things apart just so that he could put them back together. But he never did put them back together. Maria went to school, daydreamed, and got A's or F's, depending on her interest level. Many classes were easy, but others were boring, and she often didn't hear important instructions and information. Maria was told that she was lazy and absent-minded; that she didn't pay attention or didn't try hard enough; that she was stupid. When Maria was 40, she realized that she, like her brother, had ADHD.

Maria's son was diagnosed early because he screamed. He screamed with frustration and stress. On the other hand, Maria's father, who at age 69 wrote, "Life itself is the heaviest burden," was never diagnosed.

Attention Deficit Hyperactivity Disorder (ADHD) is a behavior disorder that affects children and adults. It diminishes a person's ability to selectively pay attention—to attend to what is important and to ignore what is not important or relevant. People with ADHD also lack the ability to stay focused and the ability to shift or resume focused attention. A child with ADHD switches from one activity to another, but rarely finishes anything. He or she responds eagerly to almost everything, is upset easily, and reacts quickly and impulsively. He or she can be delightful and charming but often "doesn't know when to stop." A child with ADHD cannot read social cues. For example, the child may annoy or irritate peers by interrupting, pushing into a line, or poking too often or too hard. ADHD children usually have problems getting along with others, doing chores, turning in homework, and concentrating in school. Children with ADHD are often unable to:

- consider consequences
- pick out important details
- work through the decision-making process or evaluate options
- problem-solve
- refrain from reacting impulsively
- remember, especially more than one step in a series
- remain on task and finish what was started
- notice social feedback cues.

What causes ADHD? There is clear medical evidence that ADHD is neurological in origin. Specific areas in the brain stem (the reticular activating system) and in the frontal cortex help control arousal and attention as well as integrate incoming information with the control of outgoing behavior. These brain areas are "underactive" in ADHD children. The neural activity in the frontal lobes of ADHD children is supressed, especially during intellectual challenge or stress. New techniques in brain imaging actually show this difference in the brain activity of ADHD children. Family stress, lack of routine, illness, and fatigue can worsen ADHD symptoms. These symptoms can also be secondary, resulting from severe anxiety or trauma, acute or chronic.

Primary ADHD is distinguished from secondary ADHD by two important factors. First, primary ADHD behaviors are present from birth or at least are noticeable by the first grade; their cause is neurological. Secondary ADHD is a behavioral-emotional response to a stressful event such as divorce. A sudden onset of symptoms indicates that a new trauma is causing the disruptive behavior. The second distinguishing feature of primary ADHD is that the behavioral symptoms occur in many environments, rather than in a specific few. Symptoms of secondary ADHD are sometimes apparent only in certain situations; the ADHD symptoms can "go away" if the stressor is removed.

ADHD runs in families. For most ADHD children, attentional disability, like most learning disabilities, is both neurologically—and genetically—based. It is important to remember, however, that there are many other causes of attentional difficulties as well. Attention problems can result from prenatal infection, trauma, or exposure to toxins—particularly alcohol, cocaine, or other drugs—or from significant injury, disease, or trauma to the brain after birth. Babies born small-for-date, prematurely, or neurologically stressed frequently have residual attentional problems. Certain medications, including those for asthma, seizures, and cancer, can significantly disrupt a child's ability to concentrate, to focus, and to sit still.

ASSESSMENT

Parental concerns are often primarily about behavior and secondly about school problems. ADHD children are frequently pushing limits, breaking rules, overreacting, arguing, and generally not listening. Parents are very often completely overwhelmed by their child's disorder and may express that they feel they are "living on the edge" or "barely surviving." Because typical discipline practices don't work, parents continually question their own effectiveness.

Between 5 and 10% of children are affected by attentional problems; boys are diagnosed three to six times more frequently than girls are. Often boys' behavior is impulsive and aggressive. In contrast, girls may appear to be lazy, unmotivated, or slow learners. ADHD children, regardless of their gender, can exhibit either behavioral extreme—a talkative, social busybody or a quiet loner, lost in an internal world of thought. Usually, teachers quickly notice ADHD children because they interrupt, make noises, and forget their homework.

ADHD children with hyperactivity often use their abundant energy disruptively. They are impulsive and lack focused, productive attention except to a few favorite activities, such as building with Legos or playing video games, pastimes that can mesmerize them for hours. The child with ADD but without hyperactivity is often mislabeled an underachiever. Often this child has a low activity level. Troubles begin at adolescence with moodiness, inappropriate emotional responses, low academic achievement, poor peer relationships, and low self-esteem.

Diagnostic Criteria

The Diagnostic and Statistical Manual of Mental Disorders, Third Edition (Revised) (DSM-IV) describes these key symptoms of Attention-

Deficit/Hyperactivity Disorder. For diagnosis, six or more symptoms of inattention and six or more symptoms of hyperactivity-impulsivity must exist for six or more months to a degree that is maladaptive and inconsistent with developmental level:

Inattention

- often fails to give close attention to details or makes careless mistakes in schoolwork, work, or other activities.
- often has difficulty sustaining attention in tasks or play activities
- often does not seem to listen when spoken to directly
- often does not follow through on instructions and fails to finish school-work, chores, or duties in the workplace (not due to oppositional behavior or failure to understand instructions)
- often has difficulty organizing tasks and activities
- often avoids, dislikes, or is reluctant to engage in tasks that require sustained mental effort (such as schoolwork or homework)
- often loses things necessary for tasks or activities (for example, toys, school assignments, pencils, books, or tools)
- is often easily distracted by extraneous stimuli
- is often forgetful in daily activities

Hyperactivity

- often fidgets with hands or feet or squirms in seat
- often leaves seat in classroom or in other situations in which remaining seated is expected
- often runs about or climbs excessively in situations where it is inappropriate (in adolescents or adults, may be limited to feelings of restlessness)
- often has difficulty playing or engaging in leisure activities quietly
- is often "on the go" or often acts as if "driven by a motor"
- often talks excessively.

Impulsivity

- often blurts out answers before questions have been completed
- often has difficulty awaiting turn

- often interrupts or intrudes on others (for example, interrupts conversations or games).

Developmental Considerations

Not all active babies or toddlers have ADHD. However, parents often describe their ADHD children as having been babies who were constantly in motion (even before birth), colicky, and difficult to get to sleep. As excessively active and impulsive toddlers, they have frequent injuries from running into walls or edges of furniture and are at risk for poisoning accidents.

Preschoolers with ADHD have more than the usual degree of difficulty playing with other children. Their impulsiveness and short attention spans disturb other children. Because they have a poor sense of their effect on others, they hug too hard, push and grab, and often hit, bite, or throw when frustrated.

When the ADHD child begins school, underachievement is common. A teacher often refers a child for intellectual-emotional evaluation because of poor organization, haphazard work, incomplete assignments, and messiness. Another frequent problem is poor peer interactions, especially in unstructured situations such as recess. During the first few years of school, intellectual testing is important to determine whether any learning disabilities also exist, so that chronic academic failure can be prevented.

Recent studies indicate that about half of children with ADHD continue to have symptoms into adolescence and young adulthood. As long as symptoms continue, treatment should continue, including medication, counseling, and education about ADHD. Untreated ADHD adolescents are at high risk for serious delinquency problems as well as school failure.

Behavioral Indicators

Most ADHD symptoms are apparent in any normal young child. The key differences between normal active behavior and ADHD behavior are:
- severity (the child's behavior often disrupts family life and classroom routine)

- pervasiveness (the child's behavior is problematic in many situations)

- early onset (lack of age-appropriate behavior control and/or attentional problems begin in early childhood, sometimes as early as infancy, although parents often do not seek help until the child is of school age).

Assessment Tools

Diagnosis and treatment involve several steps. With the older child, evaluation is more complicated because of the longer history of failure and the development of emotional, social, and academic problems. The diagnosis process includes:

- interviews with the child and parents
- behavioral evaluation through observation and checklists completed by parents and teachers
- academic review of current and past school reports
- developmental and medical history
- intellectual and emotional testing
- medical evaluation including hearing and vision
- possible further testing of language, and/or perceptual-integration by a pediatric occupational therapist.

The child's parents and teachers should complete at least one type of behavioral checklist. The Conners Behavior Rating Scale is an excellent one-page checklist. There is a separate but similar checklist for parents and teachers. The A.D.D. Behavior Rating Scale by Ned and Betty Owens is a good second checklist that scores separately ten emotional-behavioral components—inattention, impulsivity, hyperactivity, anger control, academics, anxiety, confidence, aggressiveness, resistance, and social behavior.

Begin with the child. If possible, observe the child in both a structured setting such as your office and an unstructured setting, such as your waiting room. Make a separate appointment to meet with the parents. During the initial interview, discuss their responses on the behavior checklists. Ask about the following areas to uncover the history of the problem behaviors:

- *Developmental history.* At what age did symptoms begin, and to what extent did they develop?
- *Medical history.* Ask about prenatal history and about any accident or illnesses (i.e., allergies, asthma, ear infections, seizures, or cancer treatment). Is the child currently taking medications that could make atten-

tional problems worse?

- *Psychosocial history.* Is there a family history of ADHD, for example, relatives who have moved from job to job, were delinquent, alcoholic? Was there a divorce in the family or an abusive or chaotic home atmosphere?

- *School history.* Was the child asked to leave a preschool or daycare placement? Is there a discrepancy between intellectual abilities and school achievement? Do other children choose this child as a friend? How often does trouble occur in or out of the classroom? Remember to ask about report cards as well as any special testing.

- *Current behavioral assessment.* Ask both parents and any major care provider to fill out the Owens or Conners questionnaire. Ask parents about their concerns, the current crisis, and how the child fits into the family. Also, ask both parents to list the child's strengths.

- *Current physicial examination.* Preferably, ask that a pediatrician who works with ADHD children and who is knowledgeable about current treatments examine the child.

- *Intellectual and educational testing.* If the school has not assessed the child's intelligence, potential, and actual academic skill levels, recommend that testing be done. Scores from the WISC-R and the Woodcock-Johnson or other ability/achievement assessment tests are essential. Remember that there is a high incidence of other learning disabilities in ADHD children. The smarter the child, the more likely that other learning problems have been "covered up."

INTERVENTION STRATEGIES

What Counselors Can Do

Parents are typically motivated to engage in treatment because of the school's concerns and the child's academic failure. Children and adolescents are generally motivated by the desire to have some friends and to stay out of trouble.

Since ADHD involves brain function, treatment of moderate or severe ADHD should possibly include medication as well as counseling, education, and environmental strategies. When treatment begins, have parents and teachers redo the behavior checklists every two weeks, and then every month. This is essential for accurate assessment of treatment.

The treatment of ADHD involves parents, teachers, school support staff, the counselor, and the physician. Even before a diagnosis is clear, intervention to ameliorate symptoms should begin. As team leader, it is your responsibility to educate the parents, teachers, child, and physician about ADHD.

Support and guide the child, parents, and teachers in their treatment decisions and plans. Help them make and prioritize a list of problem behaviors. Begin with one behavior. Make a simple, positive behavioral management plan that targets the problem behavior and has an immediate, preferably positive, consequence. The plan should include a simple way to record behavior frequency so that effectiveness can be evaluated. For example, if a big problem for the parent is getting the child to the bus stop on time in the morning with assignments, lunch, and coat, show the parents how to do a morning behavior chart. First, list the tasks that need to be completed, such as getting dressed, brushing teeth, and eating breakfast. Second, make the chart. Ask the child to contribute ideas and to do the actual construction. The chart should list the consequences (for example, five "yes" stars can be traded for a video rental). Third, arrange the environment to support the behaviors. Set out a ticking timer the child can hear and require tasks that could be done at night to be done then instead of in morning. (For example, ask the child to select clothes, prepare lunch, put everything in the backpack, and place the backpack by the door before going to bed.)

Assist with educational planning by being the child's advocate. Help the family obtain appropriate special education services if disability criteria have been met. Help the family members understand the functions of specialists (special needs teacher, school counselor, nurse, language therapist, occupational therapist, and physical therapist) and how to evaluate IEP's (individual educational programs). Teach the family about medications and encourage frequent communication with the child's physician.

Finally, provide emotional-behavioral counseling.

The long-term counseling goal is to address the emotional problems. The parents and the child often feel frustrated and humiliated because of repeated failures. Parents that have experienced their child being "kicked out" of school—even preschool or daycare—either feel hopeless, guilty, and inadequate or have become angry. Address these feelings.

Stimulant Medication

Often the most successful treatment begins with stimulant medication. With appropriate dosage levels, about 70% of children show significant improvement. Recent studies indicate ADHD adults also benefit from medication. When medication is effective, changes that appear include decreased impulsivity and hyperactivity, diminished aggression, and increased attention span. Information about the several different drugs used to treat ADHD is included in the resources listed at the end of this chapter. Encourage parents to learn about how and why medication can make a difference in their child's life.

Two weeks after medication is started, checklists need to be repeated. Scores should show that the child exhibits more goal-directed behavior; more focused attention, lasting until task completion; a less hurried demeanor; more ability to stop and think before responding; and an attitude that is more positive, less frustrated.

The child should not seem lethargic or drugged. Energy levels should be good. Fragility of emotions (bursting into tears for little reason) means that the current level of medication is inappropriate or that the child is not metabolizing one dose before receiving the next. (The child is on a roller coaster of on-off within one day.) Consult with the physician about smaller doses given more often. If improvement is slight, dosage level usually needs to be increased, or sometimes a change in medication is warranted. After each change, behavioral checklists need to be repeated.

After a month of correct medication and other counseling interventions, the child, parents, and teachers should enthusiastically describe improvements in peer and social relationships, academics, attitude, and self-esteem.

Once there has been significant improvement and the medication is working, the child can focus, remember, and put to use whatever is being taught. This is time to introduce more information about ADHD and to try new environmental strategies. Just as a diabetic child and family learn about diabetes to control the disease, the ADHD child and his or her family need to learn about ADHD. Encourage the child and parents to read about ADHD, so that they will come to understand causes and treatments of ADHD and become their own best advocates.

What Parents Can Do

Emphasize these important rules to the parents:

- Start by assigning tasks that the child will likely master, so that he or she has the opportunity to experience success.

- Increase expectations by small achievable steps. (For example, give the following task: *Before school, take medication and be ready for the bus with only one reminder.* After a week or two of success, add something such as *Brush your teeth* or *Make your bed.* Be sure to add just one task at a time.)

- Have a visual chart of rules, chores, and rewards.

- Reinforce improvements with checks, hugs, and praise.

- Have consistent routines for everything. (For example, tell the child that homework time is 30 minutes after supper.)

- Be predictable. (Say, for example, If you don't do homework one day, there is no TV the next.)

- Be positive. (Say, for example, that if the child completes the homework one day, there is free-choice TV for one hour the next day.)

- Talk only after you have established eye contact with the child.

- Be brief and specific when giving directions and make no more than one request at a time.

- Ask the child to tell you what was heard and remembered.

- Set rules and enforce them. Avoid debates.

- Avoid physical punishments. They are ineffective and teach inappropriate behavior.

- Prepare a child for transitions.

- Avoid overstimulation.

- Prepare for fatigue and medication "wear-off" at the end of the day.

Parents of very active infants should try to maintain body contact by hold-

Table 4.1 ADHD Medications Summary

Type	Actions	Utility	Advantages	Disadvantages	Medications
Stimulants	May increase levels of neurotransmitters in the synaptic junction. (One theory of ADD causation is the lack of enough neurotransmitters, especially in attention-focus parts of the brain.)	Most consistently helpful class of medication. Work for hyperactivity, inattention, and impulsivity.	Usually effective; widely available; most practitioners familiar with their use. Many dosage forms available.	Considerable cultural prejudice against stimulant medication, especially amphetamines. May suppress appetite (usually transient, and no long-term effect on growth has been shown). Concern about sleep disturbance (but often help sleep, perhaps by allowing more organized "wind down" time in the evening).	Ritalin (methylphenidate); Dexedrine (dextroamphetamine sulphate); Cylert (pemoline).
Tricyclic Anti-depressants	May act by preventing the re-uptake of neurotransmitters in the synaptic junction, thereby prolonging their effect. May prolong the effect of short-acting stimulants.	Less universally effective than stimulants. Seem to be less helpful with inattention. Usually used with a stimulant such as Ritalin.	Long lasting (12 - 24 hours). By combining with short-acting Ritalin, may lessen need to give in-school doses—a real advantage for sensitive teens. May be especially helpful with associated depression.	Less effective alone. Can cause moodiness or tearfulness. Overdose, which causes irregular heartbeat, can be lethal.	Tofranil (imipramine).
Serotonin uptake inhibitors (anti-depressants)	Work in a manner similar to tricyclics.	Most often used with a stimulant.	Can be effective when tricyclics are not, and when stimulants alone are not enough.	Not as predictable as tricyclics; should be monitored by a physician familiar with their use.	Prozac, Zoloft, Wellbutrin.

Other medications—the utility and side effects of which must be closely monitored—include Clonidine (used to treat hypertension), lithium (used to treat bipolar disorder), mellaril (antidepressant), and tegretol or dilantin (anti-convulsants).

ing and cuddling. Swaddling the child may also prove helpful. Encourage parents to keep a routine, explaining that transition times and changes in routine are two situations difficult for the ADHD infant and toddler. Teach new parents how to recognize cues from the child that signal a need for quiet, rest, comforting, or time-out. It is crucial that parents of ADHD toddlers thoroughly childproof their home.

What Teachers Can Do

Children with ADHD are action-oriented, trial-and-error learners who learn by doing. They are most likely to stay on task when learning is novel and hands-on. They are least likely to finish anything boring or repetitive. Classroom environments that work best will include:

• structure and predictability

• shorter work periods

• small student-teacher ratio

• individualized instructions

• use of positive reinforcers and concrete, specific goals.

Behavior difficulties are likely to increase when:

• a task is multistepped or difficult

• one work period lasts a long time

• supervision is minimal

• routine is disrupted without transition time

• stimulation level in the room is high.

Effective interventions teachers can use include the following:

• Employ one-on-one communication. Stand near the child and establish eye contact, then touch the child on the shoulder or quietly say his or her name to get the child's attention. Give the child the choice of coming in when no other students are present to pre-teach new information or to review.

• Have a written system for assignments that is shared with parents. Break big assignments down into manageable segments.

Develop a regular communication system with the parents and sometimes with the counselor. Use a small notebook to send written messages back and forth between all the adults involved.

- Have a "settling down" activity after recess. Assign reading, artwork, or any quiet activity that helps the child focus.

- Make success possible. Create charts that show progress, such as the number of problems completed each day in a concrete, visual format. Have realistic goals and expectations. For example, if a child cannot handle group work, provide an alternative assignment for him or her.

- Communicate at least weekly with parents. Parents have so many complaints about an ADHD child; be sure to tell them about progress as well as early intervention with problems. Ask to be informed of any medication changes, and let parents know of any medication concerns you have.

- If daydreaming is a problem, have a code word that is understood by the child as a signal to refocus.

- List the child's strengths and create ways to build on them daily.

- Encourage participation in individual sports, such as tract and swimming.

- If tutoring is needed, consider using a high school student. Middle school children will sometimes listen better to teens. An effective tutor is often a successful ADHD high school student, who knows the problems associated with ADHD and has devised ways to cope with them. Also, this kind of tutor knows how to communicate with a younger ADHD child.

As a child advances from primary to middle grades, several changes occur in schoolwork that make learning harder. First, feedback about progress is less frequent and often less concrete. Second, teaching occurs in larger groups and is less often one-on-one, so explanations are given in lecture form. Third, assignments such as research papers are more time-consuming and are more complex. The ADHD child needs help in listing, organizing, then accomplishing each task. Finally, the completion of take-home assignments requires many steps, including remembering the assignment and the necessary materials, doing the assignment, getting the work back to school, and turning it in on time. If one step is forgotten, the homework "chain" is broken.

Successfully dealing with an ADHD child day in and day out is hard work; it requires determination and patience. Encourage parents and teachers to give frequent positive feedback to the child and also to each other.

COMMON ISSUES

Between one-half and one-third of ADHD children also have trouble with wetting and soiling both day and night. Lying and stealing are often issues, especially with the more severely affected child. Refer to Barbara Ingersoll's book listed in the Resources section for ways to cope with these problems. Encourage parents to do so also.

MEASURING PROGRESS

Rely only on behavioral questionnaires rather than on vague, generalized descriptions. Scores should reflect the degree of progress. If behavioral improvements are not evident, the treatment program or medications or both should be changed. Ask teachers about observed changes in behavior as well as academic performance.

After four to six weeks, checklists should show improvement in the child's social relationships, self-esteem, and learning at school. The number of negative and oppositional responses should decrease, and the child's disposition should be happier and more positive. The parents, the child, and the child's teacher should all feel a sense of success.

ANTICIPATED PROGRESS AND OUTCOMES

Children with ADHD are at risk for school failure and significant emotional difficulties. It is estimated that 25% of untreated ADHD adolescents break the law. If an oppositional defiant disorder or conduct disorder has developed, then the risk of delinquent behaviors greatly increases. Early identification and treatment can make a remarkable difference in all aspects of a child's life—academic performance, peer relationships, family interaction, and self-esteem.

Between 30 and 70% of children with ADHD continue to have symptoms into adulthood. The relationship between ADHD and problems during adolescence is currently being studied. It is clear that most children don't simply outgrow their symptoms. The use of medications in conjunction with behavioral management can make an enormous difference. If ADHD is making life miserable for a child, it is imperative that parents do the basics of intervention—a trial of stimulant medication, education, counseling, and behavioral and environmental interventions.

If possible, use a team treatment approach. Each member of the team—the doctor, counselor, educator, parent, and child—has a role. Each has unique information and a unique role within the group. If there isn't a team, try to create one.

ADHD children who stay in treatment with the cooperation and follow-through of their family have a positive prognosis. Children and adolescents with consistent treatment show improved mood and impulse control, lengthened attention span with less distractibility, greater frustration tolerance and stress tolerance, and the ability to organize their homework, their thinking, and their lives.

RESOURCES

Books for Parents, Teachers, and Counselors

Barkley, R. *Attention Deficit Hyperactivity Disorder: A Handbook for Diagnosis and Treatment.* New York, NY: Guilford Press, 1990.

A scholarly book that presents an overview of diagnosis and treatment for ADD. Recommended for treatment providers.

Barkley, R. *Attention Deficit Hyperactivity: A Clinical Workbook.* New York, NY: Guilford Press, 1991.

Handbook. Contains many useful forms and checklists for assessment and treatment. Also includes an excellent summary of the medications used in the treatment of ADHD.

Gauchman, R., A. Wong, and L. Shapiro. *The ADD Toolkit.* Plainview, NY: Childswork/Childplay, 1995.

For school counselors, teachers, and parents. Loose-leaf binder includes a video on ADD. Suggestions for homework assignments. Practical and accessible.

Heacox, D. *Up From Under-Achievement.* Minneapolis, MN:Free Spirit Press, 1995.

Step-by-step program with practical strategies to help children struggling in school. For parents, counselors, and children.

Ingersoll, B. *Your Hyperactive Child: A Parent's Guide to Coping with Attention Disorder.* New York, NY: Doubleday, 1990.

Easy-to-understand, practical information.

Ingersoll, B., and S. Goldstein. *Attention Deficit Disorder and Learning Disabilities: Realities, Myths and Controversial Treatments.* New York, NY: Doubleday, 1994.

For parents and teachers. Provides a wide variety of treatment options for ADD and other learning disabilities.

Jones, C. *Sourcebook for Children with Attention Deficit Disorder, A Management Guide for Early Childhood Professionals and Parents.* San Antonio, TX: Psychological Corporation, 1992

One of the few resources for preschool ages. Useful for both professionals and parents. Includes a computer component. To order, call (800) 211-8378.

Lauer, J. *Attention Deficit Disorder,* 2nd ed. Westminster, CO: Cleo Wallace Center, 1992.

Pamphlet. Provides concise summary of the diagnosis and treatment options for ADD. Available for $1 per copy from Cleo Wallace Center, a residential treatment center for children and adolescents. To order, call (303) 466-7391.

Books for Children

Galvin, M. *Otto Learns About His Medicine.* New York, NY: Magination

Press, 1988.

An intelligent and thoughtful picture book to teach younger children about ADD and the effects of medication.

Gehret, J. *Eagle Eyes: A Child's Guide to Paying Attention,* 2nd ed. Fairport, NY: Verbal Images Press, 1991.

Explains concepts of ADD to children ages nine and younger.

Gehret, J. *I'm Somebody, Too.* Fairport, NY: Verbal Images Press, 1992.

For siblings of an ADHD child.

Hipp, E. *Fighting Invisible Tigers: A Stress Management Guide for Teens.* Minneapolis, MN: Free Spirit Press, 1996.

Relevant for the child/adolescent 10 years and older who is stressed by the demands of school and the challenges of ADHD.

Levine, M. *Keeping Ahead in School: A Student's Book about Learning Abilities and Learning Disorders.* Cambridge, MA: Educators Publishing Service, 1990.

For children 10 years and older. The author uses clear language and clever illustrations to explain difficulties with memory, reading, spelling, math and attention. Includes practical strategies to assist the student. Excellent for counselors of families with LD or ADD members.

Levine, M. *All Kinds of Minds: A Young Student's Book About Learning Abilities and Learning Disorders.* Cambridge, MA: Educators Publishing Service, 1991.

Written in simple language for the younger child. Designed for parents to read aloud.

Moss, D. *Shelley the Hyperactive Turtle.* Rockville, MD: Woodbine House, 1989.

Teaches younger children about hyperactivity and suggests ways to cope with it. An entertaining picture book.

Quinn, P., and J. Stein. *Putting on the Brakes.* New York, NY: Magination Press, 1991.

For younger children. Describes ADD.

Shapiro, L. *Sometimes I Drive My Mom Crazy, But I Know She's Crazy About Me.* Plainview, NY: Childswork/Childsplay, 1994.

Storybook that incorporates common treatment strategies used by counselors. Humorous.

Videos

It's Just Attention Disorder
by Dr. Sam Goldstein

An excellent video to help children with ADHD understand the disorder and learn what they can do for themselves. Particularly good for children who have difficulty reading. Available from the Neurology, Learning and Behavior Center, 230 South 500 East, Suite 100, Salt Lake City, UT 84102. (801) 532-1484.

ADHD: What Can We Do
by Dr. Russell Barkley

Provides an overview of the most effective approaches to treating the problems associated with ADHD. Recommended for parents. Available by calling ADD Warehouse: (800) 233-9273.

ADHD: What Do We Know
by Dr. Russell Barkley

Presents the lives of several children with ADHD and their families. Recommended for parents, teachers, and children. Available by calling ADD Warehouse: (800) 233-9273.

Agencies and Organizations

Attention Deficit Disorder Association, ADDA
1788 Second St., Suite 200
Highland Park, IL 60035
National support association for parents of children with ADHD.

ADD Warehouse
300 NW 70th Ave., Suite 102
Plantation, FL 33317
(800) 233-9273

Free catalog of books, tapes, charts, and handouts on ADD.

CHADD: Children with Attention Disorders
8181 Professional Place, Suite 201
Landover, MD 20785

The largest national advocacy group for families with ADD. Instrumental in changing some of the laws and identifying ADD as a legitimate disability. Over 100 support chapters. Call 301-306-7070 for the one nearest you.

KIDSRIGHTS
8902 Otis Avenue
Indianapolis, IN 46216
(800) 892-KIDS

Publishers of books and videos addressing ADHD and other problems. Free catalog.

CHAPTER 5

Learning Disabilities

"I hate school," Cheryl, a second-grader, blurted out as soon as the group session started.

Her friend, Carrie, nodded in agreement and then spoke barely above a whisper. "School gives me headaches. It's way too long. I'm slower than the others are, so I have lots of homework. Some kids have LD. That means they don't think fast. I don't have LD; I just work slow."

Children and adults need to experience success to feel competent and worthwhile. Repeated failure destroys confidence and the willingness to try. For children, to whom school is so important, failing in school is tantamount to failing in life. Children who underachieve in school may give up on their goals and her dreams, and even on themselves. When children experience one disappointment after another—failing test after test—their response is to quit, to leave emotionally or physically, to act out, or to pretend they don't care. These children are at high risk for becoming dropouts, class clowns, and delinquents. Many of these children are learning disabled—LD for short. These children learn differently.

It is estimated that 10 to 20 % of children in the United States need specialized education because of learning difficulties. Three out of every four are boys. Often, more than one factor contributes to a child's academic difficulties, especially if failure has been chronic. Hereditary factors account for a large proportion of cases, particularly reading disabilities and ADHD. Familial recurrence rates for dyslexia range from 35 to 45 % compared with a population base rate of 3 to 10 %. Recent brain structure research indicates that both dyslexic and ADHD children show specific deviations from normal patterns of brain symmetry.

Any trauma to the brain, such as infection or hypoxia, before, during, or after birth, can result in learning problems. Learning problems can also result from several prenatal circumstances, including being exposed to alcohol (or other harmful substances); having a teenage mother (pregnancy complicated by poor eating habits); or having a mother who, during pregnancy, smoked heavily or had diabetes or toxemia. If a child was premature, born small-for-term, or had low birth weight, the child is at risk for learning problems. Other causes may be medical, such as treatment for cancer, especially irradiation of the head.

Emotional traumas can also result in learning difficulties. Chronic abuse or neglect, including sexual abuse, can interfere with intellectual development. Whatever injures the brain—emotionally or physically—hurts learning.

What is a learning disability? There are several common, recognized learning disorders. These affect reading, mathematics, writing/spelling, and general academics. These disorders are not mutually exclusive. A child can have one or all of them. Nearly half of all school-age children with other disabilities (physical, emotional, or behavioral) also have learning difficulties.

There are six basic forms of learning disabilities that affect children:

1. *General Academic Disability.* Students have trouble with most academic subjects but have good social skills and common sense and may be good athletes.

2. *Language Learning Disability.* Students have trouble understanding or remembering what they hear. They have good ideas but have trouble finding the right words to express them. They often misunderstand or never even hear a lot of what is explained in the classroom.

3. *Visual Perceptual Motor Disability.* Students may have trouble with several very different tasks. Handwriting might be difficult, slow, and messy. Spelling (visual memory) can be significantly impaired. Reading may be slow; remembering what was read is difficult.

4. *Developmental Arithmetic Disorder.* Complex thinking can be affected by problems with verbal reasoning and logic. A child may have difficulty understanding math concepts, reading symbols, or remembering facts.

5. *Social Perceptual Disability.* Students don't understand the social signals

given to them by other students.

6. *Attention Deficit Hyperactivity Disorder (ADHD)*. Up to 40 % of students with LD also have ADHD. Children with ADHD have difficulty sustaining attention; attending to important information; ignoring irrelevant information or stimuli; organizing and completing tasks; and controlling impulsive reactions.

ASSESSMENT

When a child is underachieving or failing, the primary counseling goal is to determine whether an undiagnosed learning disability exists. It cannot be overemphasized that when school failure is not treated, the child's prognosis is poor. Chronic academic failure produces emotional distress, loss of self-confidence, discouragement, depression, anger, and decreased effort— all of which can lead to the child dropping out of school.

Diagnostic Criteria
Academic, Developmental, and Medical History

Review all past educational and intellectual assessments. A learning disability is reflected by a significant scatter of high and low subtest scores on standard I.Q. testing and is evident when academic achievement does not reflect intellectual ability. Each state has specific scoring criteria that must be met for a child to be diagnosed as LD and become eligible to receive educational assistance.

Review present and past school records, including report cards and achievement test scores. Look for trends and sudden changes, and for areas that have been strengths as well as problems. Pay attention to teachers' comments about behavior, attitude, and relationships with peers. Also note frequency and patterns of absences. Speak to the child's teacher directly and ask about the child's strengths and weaknesses.

Ask parents to complete a developmental/behavioral history questionnaire. Look for delays in developmental milestones as well as any patterns of behavioral problems.

Assess social and family history, noting any family history of learning disabilities. Most learning disabilities are genetically based but are undiagnosed. Ask if anyone in the immediate or the extended family had difficulties in school.

Request that parents complete a Childhood History Form such as Goldstein and Goldstein's and review medical information about prenatal, perinatal, and early childhood health. Note any medical problems such as prematurity, asthma, cancer, diabetes, seizures, and chronic ear infections that could disrupt learning. It is important to have a complete medical-developmental history.

Ask about recent medical evaluations or problems. Ask about the presence of "soft" neurologic signs and/or recurrent problems such as allergies, headaches, or attentional problems. Ask whether the child is taking any medications; many have side effects that disrupt attention, concentration, or memory.

Emotional/Intellectual Evaluation

Intellectual ability and achievement assessment includes the Wechsler Intelligence Scale for Children and the Woodcock-Johnson Psychoeducational Battery, Revised. School psychologists increasingly use the Kaufman Assessment Battery for Children (K-ABC) to measure both ability and achievement. Ask the school counselor to explain the school's interpretation of test results.

One of your roles is to help parents ask questions about their child's test scores. Only professionals who regularly administer tests fully understand the significance of the results. Assist parents and children in translating the professional assessment into meaningful information.

Learning disabilities involving reading and writing indicate underlying problems with perception and visual-motor skills. A pediatric language specialist (speech pathologist) and a pediatric occupational therapist should do the evaluations. The two most common tests are the Bender Visual Motor Gestalt and the Developmental Test of Visual Motor Integration.

Evaluate emotional-behavioral problems that complicate or are secondary to learning disabilities. Have the child, parents, and teachers complete behavioral-emotional rating scales about the child. Projective tests give helpful insights into the child's feelings about self, family, and peers.

Developmental Considerations

If an older child has never been diagnosed learning disabled, don't assume he or she isn't, especially if a behavior-problem referral includes poor school achievement. Children camouflage learning problems; they use acting-out behaviors to avoid looking stupid. They learn to compensate by becoming the class clown, or they find ways to pass tests even when they don't understand the material. The brighter the child, the longer the cover-up can continue. I once tested an intellectually gifted child who was failing third grade. He couldn't read, but nobody knew it. He sobbed with relief after I uncovered his secret and explained to him that he wasn't stupid or lazy; he was dyslexic.

Early diagnosis can mean early intervention. Preschoolers, toddlers, and infants should have developmental screenings done as part of well-child care. Ask parents whether their child has ever received a developmental evaluation and, if so, whether their physician expressed concern about development. Delays in fine motor, visual-motor, or language skills are often indicators of future learning difficulties. Periodic developmental screening to detect delays is important, especially since the passage of Public Laws 99-142 and 99-457. These two laws require that all states provide an appropriate education to children over three years of age regardless of handicapping condition.

Early signs of possible future learning difficulties do exist. Ask every parent about these developmental warning signs:

- *Was the child's language development delayed?* Does the child have a current speech problem? By three years of age most of what a child says should be understandable. Speech delays can be predictors of reading delays. Language concerns should be evaluated by a speech pathologist that specializes in children.

- *Is the child clumsy, weak, or poorly coordinated, or does he or she have poor muscle tone?* If so, motor-perceptual processing may be a problem and should be evaluated by a pediatric occupational or physical therapist.

- *Does the child have a short attention span?* By age five, a child should be able to sit quietly and listen to a story. If attention is a problem, review the chapter on ADHD.

• *Is there a discrepancy between the child's ability and achievement in school?* As schoolwork becomes more complex, a child with a learning disability does less and less well.

Behavioral Indicators

One survival response of a child to academic failure is to cover up feelings of frustration and shame with a behavioral "mask." Examples include the know-it-all, the class clown, the helpless whiner, or the chronic under-achiever. Another survival response is to join an alternative group. Still another reaction is to drop out of school and/or to act out anger and shame through delinquent behaviors involving alcohol, drugs, cars, and sex.

Most LD children are initially referred for counseling not because of suspected learning problems but because of other troubles. (Often the referral is made after a parent-teacher conference.) The most common secondary reasons are:

• negative attitude and attention-seeking behaviors (the child is disruptive in the classroom and is given the diagnosis of adjustment reaction, depression, ADHD, or predelinquent)

• stomachaches and headaches (the child doesn't want to go to school or stay in the classroom and is frequently absent)

• school phobia, disinterest, or fears

• underachievement

• difficulty with one subject (the child overgeneralizes and says "I hate school" or "I'm dumb" because of an inability to succeed in one subject)

Assessment Tools

A complete assessment includes evaluating all six aspects of a child's functioning—intellectual, perceptual and visual-motor, academic, behavioral, emotional, and medical. See Tables 5.1 and 5.2 for descriptions of some recommended diagnostic tests.

Table 5.1 **Intellectual Evaluations**

	Intellectual Evaluations	
Cognitive Abilities	**Academic Achievements**	**Neuropsychological Tests**
• Wechsler Intelligence Scale for Children • Kaufman Assessment Battery	• Woodcock-Johnson Psychoeducational Battery • WRAT — Wide Range Achievement Test • Peabody Individual Achievement Test	• Halstead-Reitan Battery for Children • Luria Nebraska Child & Adolescent Test Battery

Table 5.2 **Other Diagnostic Tools**

Perceptual, Visual Balance and Fine Motor Abilities	**Large Motor Movement, Coordination, and Balance**	**Behavior Rating Scales**
• Bender Visual Motor Gestalt • Evaluation assessment by a pediatric occupational therapist	• Evaluation assessment by a pediatric physical therapist	• Conners Parent and Teacher Rating Scales • Yale Inventory • Child Behavior Checklist • Achenbach Child Behavior Checklist

INTERVENTION STRATEGIES
What Counselors Can Do

Evaluation. Every child with school failure or underachievement should have a full evaluation—emotional (especially for depression), intellectual, and academic. The academic evaluation begins at school and should include evaluation of both ability and achievement. Be sure to look at all the reasons that a child is not succeeding in school before you begin an intervention plan.

Advocacy. Following assessment, your next role is to be the child's advocate at school. Discuss and explain testing information and educational plans with the child and parents. Counsel the child and parents about what the scores mean. Assess whether therapy and educational intervention are appropriate and sufficient. Attend school staffing meetings, especially when the Individual Educational Programs (IEPs) are being discussed and created.

Educational counseling. An important intervention task is educational counseling of parents and child. Explanation of the child's particular learning disability in simple language is key. Understanding LD gives both parents and child the knowledge and confidence to work with educators to create an effective remediation program. A child with a learning disability has probably felt stupid or retarded and is embarassed to ask, "What does this report mean? What do these scores say about me?" Understanding is also developmental. This means that a six-year-old can begin to understand the learning disability but will need more information as he or she gets older.

Team development. Teach the concept of team cooperation. The child, the parents, the teachers, and the counselors must all work together for the child's success. Be specific about what each team member's job is. For example, the teacher decides on learning/homework strategies. The student completes and turns in homework. The parent reviews assignments daily and reports success or failure to the child's teacher and therapist on a regular, frequent schedule.

Management. Management often means long-term involvement. Your work as the counselor will depend on the resources of the family, school, and community. Learning disabilities do not go away. A child learns ways to cope and compensate, and this takes time. Be sure a child understands that being learning disabled does not mean being stupid. Encourage different ways of expressing feelings, such as journaling, drawing, playing sports, and playing music. Encourage the child to talk about the frustrations of coping with a disability. Ask the child what he or she wants out of therapy. Often the answer is something like, "I want my parents off my back," or "No homework." Try to establish a rapport with the child by working with him or her on one of the stated goals.

Prevention of secondary problems. Preventive counseling is ideal. Refer to the counseling goals listed in the "Giftedness" chapter.

What Parents Can Do

Because the parents are the daily link between the child and school, they are the key to making educational interventions work. Written communication between teacher and parents should take place daily by using a notebook that is sent back and forth. Both parents and teachers should initial daily assignments, include any pertinent information, describe specific examples of behavior, and recount at least one success. Ask that parents also communicate specifically and regularly with the child, the therapist, the tutor, and anyone else that is involved.

Encourage parents to identify their child's strengths and to help their child develop these strengths. Advise parents not to take away a child's opportunities for success in areas such as sports practice, art or music lessons, or scouting as punishment for poor grades or lost homework.

Help the family establish a study routine. The following guidelines have proved effective:

- Homework time should be part of the evening routine; after school a child needs to rest, eat, and play before beginning homework.

- Time, location, and length of study time should be established and adhered to.

- Parents should look over the assignments, help the child organize materials, and set a length of time for working on each assignment.

- Begin with the hardest subject first.

- Encourage the child to take 5- to 10-minute breaks every half-hour.

- Enforce the rules (such as no TV and no phone calls) until study time is finished.

- Praise and reinforce successful behavior.

Remind parents that the more interest they show, the more inclined their child is to complete his or her homework. Remind them, too, that when homework is finished, they must check that the child has put it in the backpack that is carried to school. Many LD kids do homework and then lose it or forget to turn it in.

What Teachers Can Do

Work with the school on "bypass and success strategies"—ways to make learning easier, more efficient, successful, and fun. If a child can't remember the multiplication tables, ask the teacher to let the child use a calculator (while he or she continues to memorize). If a child can't spell and labors over the physical act of writing, let him or her use a keyboard or a computer with a spell-checker.

The key is agreeing on what really needs to be learned. What are the steps to learning it? What are other ways of learning, and of demonstrating the degree of learning, besides the traditional approaches of testing, writing reports, or doing practice sheets? Taking untimed or oral tests allows a child to show a teacher what is actually being learned. Use of computers as an examination strategy is another alternative.

As the therapist, determine whether remediation of basic skills is needed. If a skill level in reading or math is below grade level, suggest that the child be tutored. Peer tutoring is often successful. A student with similar learning difficulties who has learned how to cope successfully is often the best tutor.

An important catch-up time is summer vacation. Children with learning problems tend to stay away from libraries and avoid reading and math programs. Ask teachers to help design simple and fun summer learning plans.

As the child's advocate, don't let the child be humiliated; overexposure to criticism is detrimental. Write letters or talk to the child's school principal if necessary. Assist with creating positive intervention where it's needed.

ANTICIPATED PROGRESS AND OUTCOMES

Learning disabilities do not go away. Just as for any chronic illness, intervention for learning disabilities must be reviewed and revised. The stakes are high. Children with learning disorders can become depressed and angry and act out or drop out. Early and appropriate intervention means a child can learn ways to cope and compensate.

RESOURCES
Books for Parents, Teachers, and Counselors

Benson, P., J. Galbraith, and L. Espeland. *What Kids Need to Succeed.* Minneapolis, MN: Search Institute and Free Spirit Press, 1995.

Summarizes the results of a large, nationwide study. Describes 50 assets young people need to experience personal success. Identifies ways parents, teachers, and counselors can help children develop these assets. Emphasizes what families can do to improve their children's future.

Fisher, B., and R. Cummings. *When Your Child Has LD: A Survival Guide for Parents.* Minneapolis, MN: Free Spirit Press, 1995.

Explains the five types of LD in accessible, lay language. It describes a child's legal rights and includes resource listings and recommended readings.

Gaddes, W., and D. Edgell. *Learning Disabilities and Brain Function: A Neurological Approach.* New York, NY: Springer-Verlag, 1993.

For professionals. Combines theoretical orientation, practical suggestions, and pertinent case studies in an integrated, multidisciplinary approach to treating learning disabilities in adults and children.

Ingersoll, B., and S. Goldstein. *Attention Deficit Disorder and Learning Disabilities: Realities, Myths and Controversial Treatments.* New York, NY: Doubleday, 1994.

For parents. Informative, accessible, and timely information.

Levine, M. *Keeping Ahead in School: A Student's Book About Learning Abilities and Learning Disorders.* Cambridge, MA: Educators Publishing Service, 1990.

For parents to read to their children. In clear language and through clever illustrations, the author explains difficulties with memory, reading, writing, math, and attention. Includes practical strategies to use to assist the student.

Nowicki, S., and M. Duke. *Helping the Child Who Doesn't Fit In.* Atlanta, GA: Peachtree Publishers, 1992.

A guide for the child who doesn't understand or who uses nonverbal communication. Also offers skills that children can practice. For counselors, teachers, and parents.

Winebrenner, S. *Teaching Kids with Learning Difficulties in the Regular Classroom.* Minneapolis, MN: Free Spirit Press, 1996.

New book from the author who wrote the classic, *Teaching Gifted Kids.* For teachers and counselors.

Books for Children

Cummings, R., and G. Fisher. *The School Survival Guide for Kids with Learning Differences.* Minneapolis, MN: Free Spirit Press, 1994.

Explains LD in terms that young children can understand and gives teachers tools for children. Also available in Spanish and on audio tape.

Cummings, R., and G. Fisher. *The Survival Guide for Kids with LD.* Minneapolis, MN: Free Spirit Press, 1994.

Describes the different learning difficulties and emphasizes a positive treatment approach. Also available in Spanish and on audiotape.

Gehret, J. *The Don't Give Up Kid.* Fairport, NY: Verbal Images Press, 1990.

A warm story about a child with a learning disability.

Janover, C. *The Worst Speller in Junior High.* Minneapolis, MN: Free Spirit Press, 1995.

A fictional story about a seventh-grader with dyslexia who longs to be a popular kid, despite her spelling problems. Recommended by ALA *Booklist.*

Lasker, J. *He's My Brother.* Minneapolis, MN: Free Spirit Press, 1990.

A picture book for children younger than seven that encourages siblings and friends of children with learning disabilities to be more understanding.

Levine, M. *All Kinds of Minds: The Young Student's Book About Learning Abilities and Learning Disorders.* Cambridge, MA: Educators Publishing Service, 1991.

Written for the young elementary child with learning disabilities. Designed for a parent to read to the young child.

Roby, C. *When Learning Is Tough: Kids Talk About Learning Disabilities.* Minneapolis, MN: Free Spirit Press, 1994.

Eight boys and girls tell what it is like to live with their particular disability; they share their struggles as well as their talents and hopes for the future.

Schumm, J., and M. Radencich. *School Power: Strategies for Succeeding in School.* Minneapolis, MN: Free Spirit Press, 1995.

Hundreds of how-to tips to improve school performance. Includes reproducible handouts. For children 11 years and older.

Agencies and Organizations

Free Spirit Press
400 1st Avenue North, Suite 616
Minneapolis, MN 55401-1730
(800) 735-7323

Specializes in self-help books for gifted children and for children with learning differences.

Academic Therapy Publications
20 Commercial Blvd.
Novato, CA 94949-6191
(415) 883-3314

Learning Disabilities Association (LDA)
4156 Library Rd.
Pittsburgh, PA 15234
(412) 341-1515

Most states as well as many regions have LDA chapters. The national organization can help you locate the one nearest you.

Council for Exceptional Children
1920 Association Dr.
Reston, VA 20191-1589

American Academy of Pediatrics
Department of Publications
141 Northwest Point Blvd.
P. O. Box 927
Elk Grove Village, IL 60009

National Center for Learning Disabilities
381 Park Avenue South, Suite 1401
New York, NY 10016
(212) 545-7510

Center for Best Practices in Early Chilhood
Western Illinois University
27 Horrabin Hall
Macomb, IL 61455
(309) 298-1014

CHAPTER 6

Giftedness

"Why can't I put a bookmark in my dream?" asked five-year-old Margaret.

Gifted children are different, and being different is a challenge. For some gifted children, their giftedness is a handicap and means isolation and self-doubt, even self-loathing. Education, counseling, and emotional support for gifted children and their parents are as important as education and support for any child who is different or disabled.

In 1993, the U. S. Department of Education's *Report on Gifted Children and Education* criticized public schools for neglecting the country's approximately two million gifted children. Too many children sit in classes intellectually unchallenged; only 27 states require schools to offer special educational services for gifted students. Regardless of what a school offers, the classroom teacher can either frustrate or nurture a bright child. However teachers, as well as schools and our society in general, often do not recognize gifted children as having special educational or emotional needs.

Being gifted does not automatically mean being successful or well adjusted. In *Guiding the Gifted Child,* Webb, Meckstroth, and Tolan present research that indicates that many gifted children are underachievers. The authors stress that many talented children perform far below their intellectual potential and are at risk for quitting school and for committing suicide. (It is estimated that as many as 15 to 30 % of high school dropouts are intellectually gifted.) Another concern is depression, which is a frequent problem for gifted persons. Webb, Meckstroth, and Tolan suggest three reasons for depression in bright children:

• Gifted children are powerfully motivated to live up to impossibly high self-imposed standards of morality and achievement.

- Gifted children often feel different and alienated from others.

- Gifted children often have an intense concern about the problems of human existence.

When researchers asked gifted children about their frustrations, there was agreement on several issues. A counselor should use these concerns to check out key "gifted issues" with a child. In *The Gifted Kids Survival Guide,* Judy Galbraith describes them as follows:

- Adjustment to school. Gifted children ranked adjustment to school as the number one problem. Gifted children experience school as too easy, too boring, and repetitive. Also, these children have to deal with teachers who get angry when challenged.

- Peer relationships. Classmates often tease gifted children about being smart.

- Adult expectations. Gifted children feel that adults expect them not only to be smart at everything, but also to behave well all the time.

- Friendships. Gifted children find it difficult to meet other children who have similar interests and who think in similar ways.

- Self-esteem. Gifted children often feel different, alone, alienated—even dumb.

- Understanding giftedness. Gifted children often do not understand their gift; no one really explains what being gifted means.

ASSESSMENT

Who are the gifted? About three children in every 100 have an IQ of 130 or above. That means about one child in each classroom. Schools determine giftedness in a variety of ways. The three most commonly used assessment methods are group IQ tests, achievement tests, and a combination of teacher-parent recommendations.

Diagnostic Criteria

Linda Kreger Silverman in *Counseling the Gifted and Talented* has described the special needs of gifted children. The presence of each of the following characteristics should be assessed in each gifted child:

1. *Asynchronous development*. Silverman emphasizes that giftedness means asynchronous development because "advanced cognitive abilities and heightened intensity combine to create inner experiences and awareness that are qualitatively different from the norm." This asynchrony means not having intellectual, emotional, physical, and social growth in sync or parallel with each other; it creates inner tension and produces frustration. For example, a five-year-old gifted child may think like a ten-year-old but react emotionally like the young child that he or she is; adults are confused by this dichotomy.

2. *Extra perception*. Just as the musician hears the difference between a note played correctly and one played off-key, the bright youngster is often sensitive to small differences, whether the medium is language, art, social action, or rules and behavior. To such children, small differences are very important, a trait that can frustrate the people around them.

3. *High involvement*. An obsession with ideas is a hallmark of gifted children. They become curious about an issue and cannot truly rest until they get an answer. Their peers are unable to understand the fixation and respond to it by telling the gifted child to "lighten up."

4. *Supersensitivity and exceptional empathy*. Gifted children often feel concern and compassion to which they cannot respond. For example, a gifted child sees a homeless person and cannot understand why he or she is not allowed to bring the person home. When the child expresses this concern to friends, they either don't understand or they make fun of it. This awareness of moral, social, and emotional injustices and dilemmas also may make gifted children hold others to impossibly high standards. They may be quick to judge peers and adults who don't measure up—a trait that can put them in poor standing with teachers and other adults.

5. *Perfectionism*. Gifted children are often driven to achieve and excel; they are often unhappy and discouraged if they are not the best or do not achieve the most. It is critical for parents and teachers to soften the drive to be perfect. Children held to high standards and deprived of praise can get caught in a cycle of hopeless, misdirected perfectionism.

6. *Underachievement.* Some children react in opposition to perfectionism by refusing to follow traditional standards. Many gifted children in middle school and high school drop out due to boredom or frustration.

7. *Uneven integration of intellectual, emotional, physical, and social abilities.* Being developmentally out of sync is one problem. In addition, some gifted children's intellectual abilities are out of sync because of learning disabilities, physical disabilities, or attentional problems. If these complicating factors are present, the risk of significant frustration, depression, and low self-esteem increases.

In short, the degree of emotional and social risk is determined by how much smarter than average the child is; the degree of discrepancy between intellectual age and emotional/social age; and the number of ways the gifted child is different from peers. Risk of maladjustment also increases if a child is different because of being:

• a divergent thinker; creative; someone who has unusual insights

• a girl, especially during preadolescence and adolescence

• an ethnic minority

• physically handicapped

• learning disabled

• different looking, for example, either too thin or too fat.

Developmental Considerations

The smarter the child, the more different the child is. As the child grows older, this intellectual gap increases. The older child becomes more out of sync with peers and with his or her own social-emotional abilities. The gifted child's risk of social maladjustment and unhappiness increases with each year of growing, especially during middle and high school.

Behavioral Indicators

Use the following tools to assess depression, anxiety, self-esteem, social adjustment, and predelinquent tendencies:

• Personality Inventory for Children (PIC)

- MMPI for Adolescents

- Beck's Depression Inventory

- Conners' or Owens' Behavior Checklist (used for ADHD)

To determine IQ as well as the presence of specific learning disabilities, use WISC-III. To determine academic abilities and achievement levels, use Woodcock-Johnson.

INTERVENTION STRATEGIES

What Counselors Can Do

A preventive counseling program is ideal. The goals are to diminish or prevent underachievement, school dropout, depression, and other emotional problems. Counseling goals should include enhancing gifted children's ability to:

- understand their strengths and weaknesses

- accept themselves and nuture their abilities

- view mistakes as learning experiences

- develop conflict resolution skills

- acquire problem-solving skills

- develop an awareness and acceptance of others

- improve communication skills

- learn to be assertive but not aggressive

- develop interpersonal skills

- refine leadership and decision-making skills

- recognize and reduce stress

- use humor to relieve stress

- develop other "harder" skills, such as musical skills, artistic skills, athletic abilities, and hobbies.

The counselor must address the following needs and concerns of gifted children:

1. *Perfectionism and fear of failure.* Teachers of gifted children comment that perfectionism is the most common attribute among gifted children.

Perfectionism can become paralyzing; gifted children often are reluctant to try new things because they are afraid they will do them less than perfectly, or because they feel that making a mistake is a catastrophe. Perfectionism is frustrating and often results when brainpower is ahead of fine-motor skills. For example a gifted child may know what he or she wants to create or to build, but lack the motor skills to put it together correctly.

2. *Encourage the process, not the product.* Talk about the value of mistakes. Mistakes and failures are critical components of learning. Teach humor and the value of being able to laugh at oneself. Encourage children to read fiction, biography, and nonfiction; the stories and people in novels and biographies show how everyone—including presidents, Olympic champions, and Nobel laureates—struggles through mistakes and defeat.

3. *Hypersensitivity/depression.* When things are not going well for the gifted child, or conversely, if things are going too well, the gifted child may feel even more internal stress. This intensity can lead to depression and occasionally can even result in the child committing suicide. Teenage suicide is the third leading cause of death in the United States for teenagers. Gifted teenagers are at least as susceptible to suicide as any teenager, and some research suggests that they are more so. Aspects of being gifted that may contribute to severe depression and possible suicide include an inaccurate but increased perception of failure; increased internal or external pressure to be the best; frustration with the realization that one is not good at everything; feeling like a "weirdo" or the class nerd; and understanding the injustices and imperfections in family, friends, the community, and the world, but feeling powerless to make things better. Depression can also result from overcommitment, loneliness, dependence on extrinsic motivation, and extreme competitiveness. As a counselor, help the child sort through what's really important and what commitments can be canceled, discarded, or postponed. Help a child prioritize what is important to do now—including some of the fun activities—and what can wait. Point out to parents, as well as to the child, that everyone needs downtime.

4. *Underachievement.* There are several predictable periods in a gifted child's

life when that child is particularly at high risk for loss of motivation and underachievement. The first is when the child is in upper elementary grades and the curriculum becomes boring. The second, for girls particularly, is in early adolescence, when children often have to choose between achievement and popularity. The third is in late adolescence; many gifted children have so many talents and interests that they are unsure which to pursue. In the last period of high risk, young adulthood, some gifted people are unable to cope with less than complete success in college or adult life because there is markedly less feedback on their abilities; that is, no one is giving out report cards.

5. *Education about being smart.* In most bright children, there is a driving need to understand themselves. The counselor should offer information and suggest books (see the resources list at the end of this chapter) about the gifted.

6. *Handling stress.* Society values both conformity and innovation. Stress may come from feeling out of step with peers and from not meeting expectations. Gifted kids often expect a lot of themselves, as do the adults around them. Often these children can benefit from stress management as described by Webb, MacKstroth, and Tolan:

- *Talk about problems.* Teach children that covering up problems creates stress.

- *Remember that life is a process.* Award attempts at success as well as success itself.

- *Use decision-making skills.* Mapping out the steps for making decisions reduces the stress of decisions.

- *Take responsibility for actions.* Help children understand that blaming others doesn't help.

- *Practice simple calming techniques.* Learn relaxation strategies such as counting to ten, exercise, meditation, and controlled deep breathing.

- *Address negative self-talk.* Understand the emotional power of the irrational beliefs and messages we think to ourselves, and change this negative self-talk to positive self-talk.

What Parents Can Do

Gifted children, like all children, need to feel valued and loved for who they are rather than what they do. Encourage parents to de-emphasize the need for high achievement and the need to be good at everything. Educate parents about the importance of developing their child's talents as well as their child's nontalents; it is vital that gifted children experience being "not the best" and that they try things they may not be very good at. Suggest to parents that their child try noncompetitive sports and activities such as art, music, and dance.

Encourage parents to dilute some of their child's seriousness. Tell parents how important it is that their child learn to laugh at himself or herself and about mistakes. Humor and laughing are as important as winning or becoming the best. Teach parents to teach their child that being a kid is OK.

Emphasize that learning is a lifetime sport. Gifted children need to understand that the goal is "doing it" not "getting it done perfectly." As a model for the child, parents need to occasionally risk looking foolish or stupid and express how it feels—hard, embarrassing, but basically okay. A child needs to see his or her parents trying something they've never tried before.

Encourage parents to find gifted resources for their children outside of school. There are several valuable organizations that provide gifted children with opportunities to be with other gifted children—to think, to play, to normalize their experiences. Acceleration is not usually a healthy option; it only increases the emotional-social gap between a child and peers. Many summer camps and programs offer fun, stimulating experiences. Most universities offer special programs for gifted students.

What Teachers Can Do

As a counselor, listen to what the child expresses about the school setting, atmosphere, peers, teachers, and programs. Help the child and parents evaluate what can be changed and what is impossible to change. Then, help them ask for appropriate assistance from the teacher and school. For example, being bored at school is a serious issue; chronic boredom will eventually lead to misbehavior, apathy, and underachievement.

Ask the teacher for an opinion about the student's abilities. Ask what enrichment or gifted programs are available within and outside the class-room and whether these programs are meeting the child's academic needs. If the school does not offer any special programs for intellectually gifted students, ask the teacher if he or she is willing to make adjustments in the child's daily assignments, such as allowing the child to:

- learn at his or her own speed, especially in one or two subjects

- skip work he or she already understands

- study areas of interest beyond the regular curriculum

- take a project beyond the standard requirements so that he or she has an opportunity to be creative or more analytical

- work in small groups with other gifted students.

In a classroom the "quick learners" are often asked to help the slower students. Suggest to teachers that while some student mentoring is good, all of the child's extra time should not be used in this way.

Remind teachers that certain populations of students are often overlooked for gifted programs. For example, girls quickly learn to cover up or deny their smartness because being smart is not "cool." The handicapped are also often unnoticed because they don't "look" gifted and because their intellectual abilities may be hard to test. Gifted troublemakers often go unrecognized; bad behavior is not usually associated with giftedness, but bright kids who are bored or who are not traditional learners may amuse themselves by thinking up devious activities. The abilities of culturally different students are often underestimated because of a teacher's often unconscious bias against minority students or because the child may be learning in a second language. Intellectually different students, nontraditional learners, those who are not good at taking tests, and those who have learning disabilities, including ADHD, are also frequently overlooked.

It is important to remember that teachers aren't required to learn about giftedness. Only recently have educational classes been offered in this area. Few teachers are prepared to create their own in-class programs. Encourage parents to advocate politely and cooperatively for the educational needs of their child. If a child is gifted but unhappy in school, and changes in school are impossible, then help the child and parents look at other resources in the community. Suggest that the parents consider homeschooling. As Ben Franklin said, "Genius without education is like silver in the mine."

COMMON ISSUES

Be sure to discuss the many myths about being gifted that are often accepted by parents and teachers, such as:

• being gifted guarantees success and happiness

• being gifted means getting good grades and being a great student

• being gifted means coming from a gifted family that is successful, educated, and wealthy

• being gifted means being good at everything.

Attention from parents is frequently inadequate. Gifted children often have gifted parents who are busy pursuing their own goals and do not understand the emotional needs of their children. Because of the parents' desire to have their child excel and develop all talents, the child is often overscheduled. It is often difficult for the counselor to arrange a time for counseling, just as it is difficult for the family to reserve time for play and family fun.

During counseling sessions, gifted children tend to intellectualize their problems. Since their strength is thinking, they are often more comfortable talking about thoughts rather than feelings. If a child is also a perfectionist, it may not be okay to have "bad" feelings, such as anger, sadness, and shame.

MEASURING PROGRESS

Ask the child whether he or she feels successful and happy about:

• *School.* Is the child interested in and enthusiastic about learning? Are his or her grades adequate?

• *Friends.* Even if the child is a loner, does he or she have at least one good friend? Can the child describe at least one out-of-school activity he or she does with a friend?

• *Development of other abilities or "disabilities."* Is there a balance of activities? Can the child describe enjoyable extracurricular activities that are not directly intellect-related?

- *Perfectionism*. Can the child explain why it is okay to make mistakes and describe mistakes made? Does he or she enjoy a hobby that is not competitive?

- *Stress*. Does the child get along with his or her parents, or is the child frustrated and angry that the parents are always expecting more?

- *Self*. How does the child describe himself or herself and activities he or she enjoys doing? Can the child describe what it means to be gifted? Does the child like being gifted?

ANTICIPATED PROGRESS AND OUTCOMES

A healthy self-concept depends on family support and environmental support—the support of school and peers. To foster emotional development and a positive self-concept, and to prevent social and emotional problems, encourage gifted children to learn and talk about being gifted. As a counselor, you are the advocate, the guide, and someone with whom the child can talk. A gifted child who understands and is comfortable with his or her uniqueness can be emotionally healthy.

Gifted children are intense and are often driven to learn. They can also be delightful; they tend to ask insightful questions, to argue, and to debate. Above all, gifted children are kids. Like all kids, when they are unhappy they brag, tease, make fun of others, avoid responsibility, complain, confront, withdraw, and get discouraged. They, like all children—and perhaps even more so—need to goof off, make mistakes, laugh, waste time, play games, and relax.

RESOURCES

Books for Parents, Teachers, and Counselors

Adderholt, E., and J. Mariam. *Perfectionism: What's Bad About Being Too Good*. Minneapolis, MN: Free Spirit Press, 1995.

Defines perfectionism, describes the dangers, and explains ways to escape the perfection trap. Ages 12 and older. Thought-provoking.

Benson, P., J. Galbraith, and L. Espeland. *What Kids Need to Succeed*.

Minneapolis, MN: Search Institute and Free Spirit Press, 1995.

The result of a large national study of children, this book identifies 50 assets every young person needs to succeed. Encouraging, important news for adults to read.

Cohen, L., and E. Frydenberg. *Coping for Capable Kids.* Waco, TX: Prufrock Press, 1996.

Comprehensive guide for gifted kids, their parents, and their teachers. Contains 225 pages for parents and teachers, and 110 pages for bright students.

Kerr, B. *Smart Girls, Gifted Women.* Columbus, OH: Psychology Publishing, 1985.

Exposes the barriers to achievement that bright girls encounter and offers suggestions for parents of gifted girls.

Kerr, B. *Smart Girls, Two.* Columbus, OH: Psychology Publishing, 1986.

For parents and older gifted girls.

Schmitz, C., and J. Galbraith. *Managing the Social and Emotional Needs of the Gifted.* Minneapolis, MN: Free Spirit Press, 1985.

Over 30 concrete, easy-to-use strategies to help gifted students develop socially, emotionally, and intellectually.

Walker, S. *The Survival Guide for Parents of the Gifted.* Minneapolis, MN: Free Spirit Press, 1991.

How to understand, live with, and guide your gifted child. Recommended by Parent's Choice.

Webb, J., E. Meckstroth., and S. Tolan. *Guiding the Gifted Child.* Columbus, OH: Ohio Psychology Press, 1982.

Identifies specific emotional problems that are common among gifted children. Includes answers to frequently asked questions.

Winebrenner, S. *Teaching Gifted Kids in the Regular Classroom.* Minneapolis, MN: Free Spirit Press, 1992.

Strategies and techniques that teachers can use to meet the academic needs of the gifted and talented. Includes reproducible handouts. Recommended for teachers.

Books for Children

Blume, J. *Here's to You, Rachel Robinson.* New York, NY: Orchard Books, 1993.

Rachel is a child prodigy who has an underachieving older brother—a common dilemma for gifted children. Written directly to the middle school child.

Cleary, B. *Maggie, Maggie.* New York, NY: Murrow Junior Books, 1990.

A gifted child chooses to boycott cursive writing.

Cooney, B. *Miss Rumphius.* New York, NY: Viking, 1982.

A picture book popular with younger children about a bright, creative child.

Delisle, J. *Gifted Kids Speak Out.* Minneapolis, MN: Free Spirit Press, 1989.

Real gifted kids talk about school, friends, their families, and the future.

Delisle, J. *Kidstories: Biographies of 20 Young People You'd Like to Know.* Minneapolis, MN: Free Spirit Press, 1991.

An exciting collection of real biographies of children in today's world.

Galbraith, J. *The Gifted Kids Survival Guide.* Minneapolis, MN: Free Spirit Press, 1990.

Speaks directly to gifted children aged 6 to 10.

Galbraith, J., and D. James. *The Gifted Kids Survival Guide, II.* Minneapolis, MN: Free Spirit Press, 1992.

Designed for students aged 11 to 18. Realistic advice to gifted and talented youth on how to handle their special concerns.

Konisburg, E. *George*. New York, NY: Atheneum, 1974.
A story about a gifted boy with problems.

MacLachlan, P. *The Facts and Ficitions of Minna Pratt*. New York, NY: HarperCollins, 1988.
A gifted cello player just wants to be treated normally by her eccentric family.

Mann, P. *Whitney Young, Crusader for Equality*. Champaign, IL: Gerrard, 1972.

The autobiography of the singer and actress Whitney Young, a leader for blacks in business.

Paterson, K. *The Great Gilly Hopkins*. New York, NY: Scholastic, 1995.
Fiction. A Newberry Honor winner. A bright young girl overcomes many adversities and realizes her potential. Recommended for students who are struggling.

Agencies and Organizations

Understanding Our Gifted
Open Space Communications, Inc.
1900 Folsom, Suite 108
Boulder, CO 80302
Widely used resource for gifted children.

Prufrock Press
P. O. Box 8813
Waco, TX 76714-8813
(800) 998-2208
Catalog of resources for the gifted.

National Foundation for Gifted and Creative Children
395 Diamond Hill Rd.
Warwick, RI 02886

ALPS Publishing Co.
2985 W. 29th St.
Greeley, CO 80631-0853
(970) 330-2577

National Association for Gifted Children (NAGC)
1707 L Street NW
Washington, DC 20036

Council for Exceptional Children (CEC)
1920 Association Drive
Reston, VA 22091
(703) 620-3660

CHAPTER 7

Eating Problems and Disorders

"I remember watching Mom pack our lunches in the morning. My younger sister would get a whole sandwich with lunch meat and lots of mayonnaise, and a pack of Hostess cupcakes. My mother would then make my lunch—half a sandwhich with lettuce and tomato, but no mayonnaise. Instead of cupcakes, I'd get celery or carrot sticks. When I finished my lunch at school, I was still hungry. I knew I wasn't supposed to be hungry, but I was, so I learned to ignore my hunger. I knew something was wrong with me; I felt fat. I have since struggled with compulsive overeating and chronic dieting. Now I have a nine-year-old daughter. This morning when I was making her lunch, she said to me, "Don't put dessert in my lunch. I'm already too fat.""

In the United States, 40% of parents are so concerned about their child's eating habits that they consult with a professional about them. Typically, parents have one of two concerns—the child eats too little, or the child eats too much. Underlying these concerns are fears about obesity, compulsive eating, anorexia, and bulimia. Many parents have had their own painful experiences with weight, and many still have issues with food and eating habits. Also, they are conscious of how much our society overemphasizes body image. This concern is not unwarranted. Some distressing facts about children in the United States are:

- They are getting heavier. Statistics show that during the past 25 years, the percentage of overweight children increased from 5 to 11%. These statistics reflect the same increase reported for American adults.

- The belief develops early that being slender is ideal and that thinness is beautiful. Six-year-olds typically rate pictures of slender children more positively than pictures of chubby children. Grade school children say they would rather be disabled than fat. There are reports that 1 out of 10 preteens regularly fasts in an attempt to lose weight. Three out of 10 rigidly diet. Only 30% of eighth-grade girls feel okay about their bodies.

- In epidemic numbers children as young as eight years old are developing eating disorders.

- Eating disorders are a health problem for boys as well as girls. Fifteen percent of bulimics and binge-eaters are adolescent males. Five percent of anorexics are male.

- The discrepancy between "ideal" and "real" has increased; so has the importance of being thin. What most children deem an acceptable body is one that is virtually impossible to achieve. The average dress size of American women is 14, yet most models wear size four. Preteens admiring models in teen magazines want to be thin like them while developmentally, their bodies are responding to puberty by getting bigger, adding weight and roundness. Few teen models or TV celebrities have bodies that reflect the awkwardness and chubbiness typical of the normal preteen.

ASSESSMENT

The following are the more common concerns that often lead parents and teachers to refer a school-age child for counseling:

1. The child displays compulsive eating patterns. Parents are worried because a child is eating excessively when bored, lonely, or unhappy and appears overweight.

2. The child has been diagnosed as obese. This diagnosis means the child is more than 30% over expected weight for height and age. Determining obesity is a complex calculation that must consider the child's age, sex, type of body build, height, and developmental stage. Obesity is a medical risk as well as a significant emotional risk. Social success and academic success are also affected by obesity.

3. The child is preoccupied with food, body image, calories, fat grams, or dieting and has had dramatic weight loss that may be hidden by wearing loose clothes.

4. One or both parents have a history of an eating disorder. They are concerned that their child is repeating the pattern and pain of disordered eating.

5. There is a dramatic shift in a child's eating patterns. Adults are worried that the eating behavior—often accompanied by decreased social behavior—is a symptom of another problem, such as depression or early anorexia or bulimia.

Diagnostic Criteria

Eating disorders are a physical response to an obsession about food and physical appearance. Anorexia, bulimia, and compulsive eating have common elements. Powerful, distorted thinking drives the disordered eating patterns. School-age children, preteens, and adolescents obsessed with thinness report that they think:

• Beautiful people are thin people.

• If I am not thin, people will make fun of me.

• If I were thin, I would be popular.

• If I lose weight, I will be happy.

• There are good foods and bad foods.

• Losing weight is simply a matter of self-control; people are fat because they are weak and lack willpower.

We also know that this distorted sequence of thought is internal; it is not shared with anyone, particularly adults. Girls who are physically early bloomers are most at risk for eating problems. Other children at risk are those who are being stressed by life events, such as divorce or remarriage of parents, or a loss of a significant adult. Some girls and boys who have been sexually abused turn to binge-purge behavior as a way to deal with feelings and control issues. A food binge is one way to stifle painful feelings; the purge can become a safe way to regain control.

ANOREXIA NERVOSA

These seven physical symptoms are part of the diagnostic criteria in the *DSM* for Anorexia Nervosa:

1. *Significant weight loss or no weight gain during a normal growth spurt.* (A physician determines that the child's body weight is below 15% of the expected weight for age and height.)

2. *The feeling of being cold and chilled most of the time.* Anorexic teens often wear oversized layers of baggy clothes to hide their bodies and to keep warm.

3. *Pale and dry skin.* Chronic weight loss will also cause skin rashes.

4. *No menstrual periods* (amenorrhea). The cessation of menstruation in adolescents results from moderate weight loss and/or excessive exercising.

5. *Insomnia, moodiness, irritability.* The child exercises and then feels listless and depressed and has difficulty concentrating. (It may be difficult for parents to distinguish this moodiness from the common moodiness of adolescents.) The child is interested in doing little else besides figuring out calories and food charts.

6. *Distorted body image.* The child thinks he or she is never thin enough. The hallmark of this eating disorder is that no matter how much weight is lost, it is never enough. Looking in the mirror, the anorexic sees a fat person.

7. *An intense fear of gaining weight.* Everything about food becomes "bad and dangerous" and triggers anxiety. For example, the child may fear eating and the feeling of fullness. Some children begin to avoid their friends (who might decide to eat) and family (with whom it is expected they share meals). The anorexic child weighs himself or herself frequently during the day. Gaining even a half of a pound results in fear, guilt, self-punishments, and depression.

It is unusual for a pre-adolescent child to display any of the physical signs of anorexia. It is more common for a parent or teacher to notice these warning behaviors:

- strange eating rituals or peculiar eating behaviors, such as cutting food into tiny pieces, arranging and rearranging foods on the plate before eating, and increasingly eating fewer foods at any meal

- obsessive exercising and/or working out

- skipping meals and/or avoiding eating with family and friends

- talking more and more about hating their body, focusing on being thin, and concentrating their attention on diets, calories, and fat grams.

Anorexia most frequently affects girls between the ages of 12 and 19. During these years, huge emotional and physical changes are taking place, and girls are vulnerable to the seduction of control by starvation. Boys are vulnerable if they are competitive in sports that demand slender bodies, such as wrestling or gymnastics.

Often a child's first willingness to reconsider strict "thinning" happens when the child is scared by the negative effects from fasting. The teen may feel dizzy or disoriented and may even faint. Loss of energy, fatigue, headaches, or inability to sleep may become scary enough for the child to ask for help. If help is sought, recovery is hopeful. If the child ignores or denies these physical warning signs and resists change, successful treatment is far more difficult.

BULIMIA

The bulimic often exhibits a binge/purge cycle of eating and is often emotionally "hungry." Food eaten during a binge is usually sweet, high in calories, and easily digested. Ice cream, cookies, or cookie dough are frequent choices for bingeing. To normalize this behavior, or pretend the overeating isn't happening, the bingeing often occurs while doing something else, such as studying, watching television, reading, or talking on the phone.

The key difference between just overeating—something most people do occasionally—and a bulimic binge is the obsessive preoccupation with food and with appearance. Like the anorexic, the bulimic individual fears becoming fat and uses food to meet emotional and control needs.

The *DSM* describes several observable, identifiable symptoms of bulimia:

- Binge eating becomes a pattern of behavior with a minimum average of two binge episodes weekly for several months.

- Binge eating happens when a child feels out of control, scared, or sad.

- Binge eating sometimes temporarily gives a happy, satisfying "high" feeling.

- Purging to get rid of the food follows binge eating.
- The child shows obsessive concern for body shape and weight.

Children ages 10 to 14 may experiment with bingeing and purging as a strategy to stop weight gain. These ages are normally a period of rapid growth, during which losing weight can be a health risk. The bulimic experiment can become a habit that quickly becomes hard to break. The feeling of a full stomach becomes a stimulus for throwing up.

Like anorexia, bulimia is a medical problem that affects the patient both physically and emotionally. A pediatrician can detect signs of repeated vomiting, such as swollen neck glands, cavities on the inner side of the teeth, and dizziness from electrolyte imbalance. There is usually no weight change. The only clues to parents are the child's preoccupation with weight and calories and the child's change in eating habits. For example, the child "vanishes" to the bathroom after eating. Parents also notice sweets and other high-calorie foods missing from the pantry, perhaps at unusual hours. Recovery is possible with outpatient counseling, medications, and parental cooperation and support.

COMPULSIVE OVEREATING

Compulsive overeating involves the same set of disordered thoughts as anorexia or bulimia—an obsession with food, weight, and physical appearance. It is different from bulimia in one important way. There is no purging after the binge. As a result, this child often gains weight and is sometimes seriously overweight. With this eating disorder, the preoccupation is the experience of eating to comfort, soothe, and numb feelings. Compulsive eating is experienced equally by boys and girls and is common before adolescence. Children can learn to identify feelings and practice alternative, effective coping skills.

Developmental Considerations

A child's counselor needs to be aware that each developmental stage is marked by different problems. Clinical nutritionist Ellyn Sattor observes that "feeding is a metaphor for parent-child relationships." Her book, *How to Get Your Child to Eat. . . But Not Too Much,* describes normal and abnormal eating behaviors for each developmental stage:

Infants. The parents' task is learning the messages in their baby's crying. At this stage, the parents are in charge of what food is presented. The baby controls how much is eaten. Ideally, food is being given with love, and parents are teaching their child that eating is enjoyable.

Toddlers. Two-year-olds are oppositional and push for individuation and control. These little ones often show power by refusing food. Parents are typically concerned about what, how much, and when a child eats. Reassure parents that refusing, spitting out, and playing with food are normal behaviors. Also remind them that in food battles, there are no victors. Again, parents are in charge of the food selection and how much is presented.

Preschoolers. Preschoolers are usually easier to feed than toddlers and are not as picky. Their developmental task is mastering politeness for example, using utensils rather than fingers and learning to eat with the rest of the family. Children are learning about the relationship between food, body, and self-respect. Parents continue to have control over what, when, and how food is served, except when a child is at another adult's home, with a babysitter, or at child care or preschool.

Younger school-age children. During this stage, ages six to nine, children spend much more time away from home. Snacks and lunches are often eaten when the parents are not around, and so they no longer control much of what the child eats. There is more gender difference in how children play, how children view their bodies, and what they eat. Girls are already aware of the importance placed on being attractive and thin. Even first-graders mimic the dieting they observe at home and at school. Statistically, most children who are overweight at age nine have gained the extra weight between the ages of six and nine.

Older school-age children. The older school-age child, 10 to 13 years old, is experiencing the physical and emotional changes of puberty. These changes challenge both children and their parents. Although no one can control the timing or the types of changes of puberty, it is critical for counselors as well as parents and teachers to be comfortable with and knowledgeable about them, and send the message that these changes are healthy and normal. Table 7.1 outlines the important physical changes of puberty.

Assessment Tools

Request a medical evaluation for the child with a doctor who is knowledge-

Table 7.1 **Changes in Puberty**

Girls
- Begin between 10 and 14 years of age
- Completed in three years

8-10 years
- Estrogen and progesterone increase, affecting mood swings
- Weight gain, fat spurt before height gain

11-12 years (Range: 9.5-14 years)
- Breast buds
- Pubic hair grows
- Fat tissue around hips, buttocks, thighs create curvier look
- Voice may lower
- Menarche (average 11.5 years)

***Growth Spurt**

13-14 years (Average)
- Pubic hair and underarm hair increases
- Breasts increase in size
- Regular periods may begin
- For some girls completion of breast and pubic hair development

Boys
- Begin between the ages of 12 and 16
- Completed in four years

8-10 years
- No external body changes; continues to have the body of a child

11-12 years (Range: 9-16 years)
- Testosterone sharply increases
- Slight increase in estrogen
- Testicles increase in size
- Scrotum increases in size, hangs lower, and changes to a reddish color
- Pubic hair may begin to grow, and may be sparse
- Penis changes little
- Voice may lower

***Growth Spurt**

13-14 years (Lengthening stage)
- Testicles continue to enlarge
- Scrotum continues to develop
- Penis is noticeably longer
- Pubic hair sparse but increasing
- Voice changes

***Growth Spurt**

14-15 years (Range: 11-17 years)
- Testicles continue to enlarge
- Scrotum skin darkens
- Penis widens, glans more distinct
- Pubic hair usually develops in upside down triangle (15% of boys are still without public hair)
- Facial hair begins for some boys

*Growth Spurt for Boys and Girls
- Weight gain precedes height gain, fat spurt precedes height gain
- Girls' growth spurt is usually two years earlier than boys'
- Hands and feet grow first; torso grows last
- Nose, lips, mouth grow before head; they may appear out of proportion
- Two sides of body may grow at different rates
- Last stage of puberty means an increase in heart and blood volume
- An increase in strength and endurance follows height and weight growth

able about eating problems and who is willing to work with a counselor as well as the child and family. Ask the physician to assess the child's medical health and to determine whether the child is significantly under- or over-weight. (Weight-for-height growth charts are more likely to detect weight trend problems than weight-for-age charts.) Discuss with the physician any concerns or questions about the family's nutrition, activity level, or relevant health habits. Often advice that comes from a physician motivates families to change high-fat diets and low-activity routines. Also, if the physician advises a diet for the child, discuss your reasons for not encouraging this recommendation.

In some areas, school personnel use skin-fold calipers to measure skin-fold thickness and to estimate body fat percentage of the students. Skin-fold calipers are difficult to use accurately and are embarrassing, even humiliating, for the student. If this practice is customary at the child's school, discuss with the school counselor your reasons for wanting this practice discontinued.

Take a family history. Have the child present so that he or she can hear about the parents' experiences with physical growth, weight, and attitudes toward body image as well as past struggles with disordered eating. These disorders frequently run in families.

Important assessment tools to consider are:

- Reynolds Mood Inventory to assess depressive symptoms.

- Sentence completion to assess the child's thoughts and feelings about family, school, and self. Add sentence stems to elicit opinions about such issues as food, body image, and meals. Say to the child, for example, "When I see food, I feel. . . Family meals make me. . . When I look in the mirror, I see. . ." "The best thing about my body is. . ." "The worst thing about my body is. . ." "When someone is staring at me, I know they are thinking that. . ."

- The DRAW-A-PERSON technique to assess body image and self image.

- Rosebush visualization and drawing technique to assess self-image. (For a more complete description, see the chapter on divorce.)

- Eating attitudes survey. (Use a checklist to assess a child's feelings about many aspects of food, eating, and self-image.)

- Food log to track what the child is eating daily.
- Activity log to assess activity levels.

INTERVENTION STRATEGIES

What Counselors Can Do

When working with an eating-disordered child, develop a team that includes the child and family, a physician, and yourself. If possible, include a nutritionist or a registered dietition who can teach the parents and child about healthy food choices and about how to make incremental nutritional changes that fit their lifestyle. Strive to shift the family's focus from dieting and weight loss to eating a healthful diet, being active, and feeling good. If the child is overweight, establish a goal of growing into one's weight, rather than one of losing weight. With an underweight child, establish a goal of maintaining present weight, and help the child improve self-image, express feelings, and change his or her mindset about food.

An eating disorder is often a child's response to the desire to gain control over his or her life. Try to help the child understand why "food control" gives him or her a sense of life control and power. Encourage the child to talk about all the ways life seems out of control. Explore with the child, and then with the parents, ways in which the child can experience control and power in healthy ways. If academics are a problem, suggest a parent-teacher-counselor-child conference to problem-solve and elicit ideas. Investigate the possibility of tutoring. If friends are a source of conflict, discuss compromises. If failure is a theme, find some activity the child once enjoyed and is willing to try again, such as sports, music, drama, art, or scouting.

Teach parents and children how to recognize and be aware of the body signs of hunger and satiety. Practice visualization of fullness and hunger with a child to increase awareness. Also teach the awareness of feelings and the naming of feelings. Talk about how eating covers up unpleasant feelings. Help a child identify and name the places in the body where feelings are felt. Use role-playing, charades, or quiet imagery to pinpoint feelings in areas of the body. Also, help the child quantify the intensity of feelings. For example, a child whose brother teases about fatness feels anger in her clenched fists and hot cheeks and ranks the intensity of the anger an "8." However, when a classmate teases and calls the child a "fatso pig," that feels like a "10" right in the stomach.

Teach a child how to keep a food log, recording what is eaten; where, when, and with whom it is eaten; and the child's feelings before and after eating. Review the food log at each session and talk about healthy feelings about food. Also have a child keep an activity log. Suggest ways to make being active fun and easy (taking walks with a friend, pacing while talking on the phone, and participating informally in noncompetitive sports such as rollerblading and biking.

Once you have established rapport with a child, teach the child about the physical, medical, and emotional problems that result from dieting, fasting, and purging. Discuss the importance of being active every day. Reflect with your client about the senseless discrepancy between the size and shape of his or her own normal body and society's ideal body. Talk about how destructive it is, emotionally and physically, to try to be superthin.

Discuss with the physician and family the importance of evaluating the appropriateness of medication. Recent studies indicate that treatment of eating disorders is more quickly successful when treatment includes antidepressant medication. Depletion of neurotransmitter levels from chronic dieting causes neurological and psychological symptoms that are more quickly relieved with proper medication such as antidepressants.

Case Studies

Each type of eating disorder needs to be handled a little differently. The case studies and strategies below exemplify each of the typical eating disorders.

Anorexia. Counseling goals include identifying the child's strengths and fears and any family conflicts. Teach expression of feelings and help decrease concern about calories and weight.

Twelve-year-old Rachel had lost 20 pounds during the past six months. First Rachel and her mother were referred to a pediatrician. The doctor validated that her weight loss was dangerous. Rachel's menstrual periods had ceased, and she was suffering from irritability and insomnia. Rachel was in the early stages of anorexia. The doctor told Rachel about the dangers of anorexia and asked whether she was willing to begin eating. Rachel had been frightened by the fainting, weakness, and headaches and was willing to stop fasting. Rachel was appropriate for outpatient counseling because she was alarmed by the physical symptoms and was willing to eat and to gain weight.

In the first counseling session with parents and child, Rachel's strengths were identified, and behavioral goals for counseling were established. The counselor asked about the parents' own growth, weight, and dieting history as well as current or past family stresses.

Rachel was helped to identify ways to experience success and more control over her life. She wanted to rejoin band and try art classes. Her parents listened and agreed.

Family conflicts were identified and discussed one at a time. Some compromises were made. Rachel felt that finally her parents were listening to her. She also felt safe expressing anger and was able to cry in front of her parents. She was surprised by the support she received.

The counselor encouraged Rachel to use a notebook to write down her thoughts, feelings, and worries. Rachel found that the action of writing down her thoughts helped her to let go of worries and anger. The notebook was also helpful in marking her progress.

The counselor helped Rachel learn to recognize and to challenge critical self-talk.

Rachel's mother identified herself as a chronic dieter and often complained about her weight. She agreed to decrease these behaviors, to focus on positive self-statements, and to model a more relaxed, accepting attitude toward her body.

After ten sessions, Rachel was eating more normally, was involved in school activities, and had teased her mother for beginning another diet. She liked the increased energy, the improved mood, and the absence of the headaches she had experienced. She even felt more assertive, happy, and powerful.

Bulimia. Counseling goals are to decrease the frequency of the binge-purge cycle, increase comfort in feeling full, and heighten awareness of the difference between physical hunger and emotional hunger.

Tracy, an eighth-grader, was bingeing on ice cream and cookies in the evening when she was alone at home, especially when she was worried about schoolwork. She was purging daily by vomiting.

The counselor recommended an evaluation by a physician knowledgeable about eating disorders and took a history of the parents' and child's adolescent physical development. Was development unusually early or late? Was weight a problem for either parent? How long had the child been concerned about weight? The parents were encouraged to share their own struggles with body image when they were the child's age. (Tracy and both of her parents were early developers and felt like overgrown giants in middle school.)

Cognitive behavior strategies, which work well wth bulimia behaviors, were used, including:

- teaching Tracy to identify triggers for overeating

- helping Tracy learn to ask for help during a binge

- creating a contract with Tracy in which she agreed to limit purging behavior, to try alternative behaviors, to stay with people during and after eating to avoid purging, and ask for help when tempted to begin a binge

- explaining the binge/purge cycle (The purge drives the binge—the physical and emotional hunger brought about by the purge motivates out-of-control eating.)

- explaining that in order to decondition the purge reflex and to motivate a decrease in bingeing, Tracy needed to experience the uncomfortable stomach fullness of the binge

- teaching relaxation techniques and encouraging Tracy to practice them between sessions

- agreeing on reinforcers and rewards for decreases in the binge-purge cycle.

With the child's permission, family sessions were added. Tracy was helped to tell her parents what she needed. For example, Tracy told her mother that she was lonely and anxious during the evenings and that this was when most of the disordered-eating behaviors occurred. The mother changed her work schedule so that Tracy was less often home alone at night.

During sessions, Tracy was encouraged to practice stress management strategies such as progressive relaxation, listening to soothing music, exercising for pleasure (not weight reduction), and visualizing a "safe place." The counselor suggested that Tracy keep a journal of her feelings and thoughts. (Often the binge behavior is the only way that a child knows to soothe anxiety.) When it was appropriate, the counselor and Tracy discussed the connection between anxiety and perfectionistic goals such as excellent grades, a perfect body, and popularity.

Tracy was invited to eat during each session. First, the counselor helped Tracy practice a relaxation exercise, and then she encouraged Tracy to try—one by one—"bad" or "forbidden" foods, such as pizza or French fries. This took place at the beginning of the session so that the counselor was able to help when a purge was triggered.

During subsequent sessions, Tracy was helped to uncover ways—other than eating—to nurture herself. Some of her ideas were going to the movies, reading books, swimming, taking walks with friends, talking on the phone, and playing with her dog. Tracy realized that food had become a substitute for friendship. Her eating disorder decreased as her pleasure in other activities increased.

Compulsive overeating. Counseling goals include accepting oneself and realizing that food is used as comfort and reinforcement.

Justin was a chunky eleven-year-old boy in the middle of puberty changes. His moods were erratic, and his social skills were extremely poor. He was a loner and was teased frequently by peers about his weight, his appearance, and his knack for making weird noises. His parents complained that his compulsive eating usually occurred when he was home alone after school watching TV.

Medical evaluation confirmed that Justin was overweight and also clinically depressed with symptoms of low energy, irritability, appetite changes, oversleeping, and moodiness. Both the child and the parents were asked to describe the child's and family's strengths and problems. Several secondary emotional problems were uncovered. Justin's father had a history of depression, and Justin's parents had a history of marital conflict and had recently divorced. Justin said he felt that he did not belong anywhere. Food was effective in numbing and stifling feelings.

The counselor taught Justin the difference between physical and emotional hunger. She discussed with him how his body felt when he was full and when he was hungry. Using relaxation exercises, Justin practiced becoming quiet and listening to his body signals. Together, Justin and the counselor colored a body outline and labeled the different areas where sensations were felt. Justin was asked, "Do you remember a time when you were sad? Where did you feel it in your body? What color does sadness feel like?" Along with art therapy, sand tray and play therapy were used to identify and process thoughts and feelings that were masked by Justin's frantic eating. Through puppet play, Justin expressed that he feared losing both parents. Family meetings were crucial to reassure Justin that both parents would continue to be his parents.

What Parents Can Do

Give parents the following suggestions to encourage healthy eating habits in their children:

- Challenge the message sent by commercials, TV, movies, and videos that only thin is beautiful.

- Compliment your child on his or her looks and emphasize being healthy and strong, not thin.

- Reinforce your child's positive qualities without reference to body shape or size; focus comments on being pleased about behavior, rather than physical looks.

- Learn how boys' and girls' bodies change during puberty; be prepared to answer questions about growing out and growing up; have helpful books on puberty available for children.

- Never try to force a child to eat or not to eat.

- Don't ever put a child on a diet; don't separate one child in the family by serving only that child low-calorie foods.

- Do not use foods as rewards or consolation.

- Make mealtimes pleasant and as stress-free as possible.

- Respect food preferences, especially in an older child who may want to try being a vegetarian, for example.

- Model healthy eating patterns such as eating slowly, checking on hunger satisfaction, and making mealtime a pleasant and calm event with as few distractions as possible.

Dr. Leona Shapiro compared the eating habits of thin children to those of overweight children and found only one dietary difference—the scheduling of meals and snacks. Thinner children ate only a planned snack between meals, but fatter children snacked frequently. Encourage parents to establish healthy living habits for their family. Ensure that parents understand that any changes they make in lifestyle must affect the entire family. This policy will reinforce to all the members that the goal is health, not weight change. If menu changes are necessary—for example from high fat to low fat—be sure that all of the family members are offered the same food. (Putting one child on a restrictive diet by giving him or her "thinning" foods while the rest of the family eats "good" food sends a destructive negative message.) Encourage one menu change at a time and suggest that parents get input from their children about these changes. For example, one mother decided to offer an extra vegetable with dinner; the children took turns choosing the vegetable each night.

Changes in the amount of exercise or an activity level must also involve the whole family. Ask parents to consider exercise that everyone can enjoy. Remind them, however, that school-age children often prefer doing activities with friends. Tell parents to discuss with their children which activities would be fun to do as a family and which are more appropriate for the children and their friends.

Teach the parents how to reinforce a child's strengths without reference to body size and weight. Parents should focus on successes, wherever they happen, and remember to applaud trying. Remind parents that what's important is whether the child likes himself or herself, not what he or she looks like. If one or both parents still struggle with accepting their own body, ask them to come in for individual sessions.

What Teachers Can Do

Teachers must be aware of the growth and development issues of the age group they are teaching. Even elementary teachers need to be aware of puberty changes because some children begin puberty at age eight or nine. Teachers in the lower grades should be alert for size discrimination and weight teasing and should talk to students about the negative power of name-calling. Teachers can discuss health topics that answer questions such as: What does it mean to be healthy? Why do kids come in so many shapes and sizes? Why do we run and play at recess? Why do we eat healthful snacks?

Teachers in the middle grades can be more specific in health education. They can directly address the signs and dangers of eating disorders and discuss the many changes, including weight gain, that are part of puberty. Often, it is teachers who spot early warning signs of disordered eating patterns. The most common red-flag student behaviors observed during school are:

• not eating during lunch

• talking excessively about dieting and being fat

• counting calories and fat grams

• hoarding food

• sudden, dramatic changes in body weight without a change in height.

Some school administrators have asked young adults in recovery from eating disorders to come in and talk to the students about this issue.

COMMON ISSUES

As long as the child wants to be thin and sees "fatness" in the mirror, he or she will not change the behavior. Listen closely to the child's concerns and reasons for needing thinness, control, and power. Encourage parents to support every positive step their child makes toward healthy eating.

Set simple, realistic, achievable, and agreed-upon behavioral goals for the parents and child. Focus on skills and coping strategies, not changes in weight. If the parents are not cooperative, ask the child to talk with another adult whom the child likes and respects, such as a teacher, coach, neighbor, or relative—someone who will support your suggestions.

If the child's peer group is also involved in dieting and disordered eating, it is difficult to motivate that child to change. Peer pressure is generally given more heed than adult advice. Suggest activities that would involve a different group of children. Ask the child to agree to try a new activity.

A nonsupportive or dysfunctional family and a peer group that is powerful and focused on being thin are the two most serious obstacles a counselor faces when trying to combat a child's belief that being thin means being acceptable and loved.

ANTICIPATED PROGRESS AND OUTCOMES

Eating disorders are difficult to treat. The sooner a child gets help, the sooner the disorder can be turned around. Success is more likely if counseling is offered when the child first recognizes that trying to be thin is a destructive and possibly deadly goal. Often this recognition occurs when physical problems, such as dizziness, difficulty concentrating, or trouble sleeping begin. A child may also be ready to receive help when he or she begins to experience one or more of these losses—the loss of friendships, the loss of healthy looking hair or skin, or the loss of energy and strength.

The father's attitude is often a critical factor in the recovery of a girl with an eating disorder. If he can communicate to her that she is loved just the way she is, the child can begin to accept herself and her body.

The parent, child, and therapist should set behavioral goals early in the counseling process and then measure progress by reviewing these goals at each session. A behavioral goal can focus either on making a positive behavioral change or on decreasing negative behavior. Behavioral goals that focus on positive behavioral change include learning to eat food slowly and doing relaxation breathing between bites of food. Behavioral goals that are aimed at diminishing undesired behavior include decreasing the number of times a child checks his or her weight and finding alternatives to snacking to relieve boredom.

Medical intervention is often necessary and effective. After chronic and severe dieting, the body—including the brain—is depleted. A severe situation can be treated successfully with long-term counseling, anti-depressant medication, and if necessary, inpatient treatment.

Untreated eating disorders can result in life-long struggles with food and body image, serious physical illness, and even death. Twenty percent of college women are ashamed of their bodies and engage to some degree in binge-purge habits. Overweight young adults who continue to overeat, especially secretly and alone, suffer from feeling like ugly, unacceptable misfits and often withdraw from activities that give pleasure and purpose.

RESOURCES

Books for Parents, Teachers, and Counselors

American Academy of Pediatrics. *You and Your Adolescent.* Elk Grove, IL: Department of Publications, 1994.

Discusses nutrition and activity, how fat cells develop, and what happens in puberty. Written for adolescents; useful, too, for parents.

Berg, F. *Afraid to Eat.* Hettinger, ND: Healthy Weight Journal, 1996.

The author reports on the cultural pressures to be thin that affect children and increase eating disorders. Gives guidelines on how teachers, parents, counselors, and children can challenge cultural demands.

Brownell, K., and J. Foreyt. *Handbook of Eating Disorders.* New York, NY: Basic Books, 1986.

For professionals. Covers the basics of typical eating disorders. Good reference material for therapists.
Garner, D., and P. Garfinkel. *Handbook of Psychotherapy for Anorexia and Bulimia.* New York, NY: Harper & Row, 1985.

Comprehensive overview of the various treatment models used with eating disorders.

Hirschmann, J., and L. Zaphiropoulos. *Preventing Childhood Eating Problems.* Carlsbad, CA: Gurze Books, 1985.

For parents and counselors. Helps in prevention of eating problems at different ages.

Ikeda, J. *Am I Fat: Helping Young Children Accept Differences in Size.* ETR Associates, 1992.

For elementary teachers and counselors. Provides a variety of classroom exercises which help students realize that self image is more than body image. To order, call (800) 321-4407.

Jablow, M. *A Parent's Guide to Eating Disorders and Obesity.* New York, NY: Dell, 1992.

Recommended for parents who are worried about a child's eating habits. Describes symptoms and dangers of each disorder and outlines available treatments.

Nathanson, L. *Kidshapes.* New York, NY: HarperCollins, 1995.

A practical book for parents who are concerned about their children being overweight. Written by a pediatrician who recommends no diets for growing children.

Sattor, E. *How to Get Your Child to Eat, But Not Too Much.* Palo Alto, CA: Bull Publishing Co., 1991.

Excellent resource for parents and counselors that describes expected eating behaviors at each developmental stage. Also clearly defines the parent's role and the child's role in eating behavior.

Books for Children

Berry, J. *Good Answers to Tough Questions: About Weight Problems and Eating Disorders.* Chicago, IL: Children's Press, 1990.

Effective presentation of the basic facts about obesity, compulsive eating, anorexia, and bulimia. Good for children eight years old and younger.

Bowen-Woodward, K. *Coping with Body Image.* New York, NY: Rosen Publishing, 1989.
Helpful for middle school children. Practical information on what influences what we see in the mirror.

Declements, B. *Nothing's Fair in the Fifth Grade.* Santa Barbara, CA: Cornerstone Books, 1987.
Fiction for middle school children. A fifth-grade class first rejects the new student because she is overweight. As a group, they learn to like her personal qualities and begin to accept her. A story of hope and acceptance for an age group that can be cruel and intolerant.

Holland, I. *Dinah and the Green Fat Kingdom.* New York, NY: Dell Publishing, 1981.
Fiction. A 12-year-old girl deals with the problems of being overweight while coping with family relationships.

Holland, I. *Heads You Win, Tails I Lose.* New York, NY: Ballantine, 1988.
Story about a young girl who begins a dangerous weight-loss program while her parents are distracted by their marital problems. For middle school children.

Moe, B. *Coping with Eating Disorders.* New York, NY: Rosen Publishing, 1991.
Excellent book for middle school children and older, which describes eating disorders, symptoms, and treatment. Many stories of real children.

Newman, L. *Fat Chance.* New York, NY: G.P. Putnam's Sons, 1994.

Young adult fiction for middle school children. Poignant story of an eighth grade girl who is preoccupied with her body image.

Phillips, B. *Don't Call Me Fatso*. Austin, TX: Steck-Vaughn Co., 1991.

Fiction for the younger child. Rita is overweight and unhappy with herself. She gains control as she practices healthy eating and regular exercise.

Agencies and Organizations

National Association of Anorexia & Associated Disorders
P. O. Box 7
Highland Park, IL 60035
(708) 831-3438

The first national nonprofit organization committed to education, support, and research. Offers a newsletter.

Anorexia Nervosa and Related Eating Disorders (ANRED)
P. O. Box 5102
Eugene, OR 97405
(503) 344-1144

National nonprofit organization that distributes information about eating disorders and trains mental health professionals to work with eating disorder clients.

Anorexia Bulimia Care, Inc. (ABC)
Box 213
Lincoln Center, MA 10773
(617) 259-9767

Nonprofit organization that offers a Registry of Professionals; in each listing the individual's credentials, treatment approach, and insurance coverage is identified. Publishes a newsletter five times a year.

Eating Disorder Awareness, Inc. (EDA)
2661 Bel-Red Road
Bellevue, WA 98008
(206) 867-0700

An international program founded in 1987 and dedicated to prevention of eating disorders. Each year sponsors "No Diet Day."

CHAPTER 8

Depression

When Jeremy was asked to describe his depressed mood, he answered, "It's like I can't see colors. Life tastes like cardboard." The therapist asked Jeremy what he was doing to get out of his dark mood. He answered, "I tried lots of things for a while, but nothing helped. One day I was so down I made a list of all the people I care about and all the things I own, and matched them. . . who should get what. Then I tried to think of ways I could do it so I wouldn't make a mess." Jeremy looked down at his hands and cracked his knuckles. "I was determined to do at least one thing right in my life."

Today, children in the United States have a 40% chance of being treated for major depression during their lifetime. Untreated depression disrupts learning, concentration, eating, and sleeping. It also affects relationships with parents, teachers, and peers. Untreated depression can lead to suicide, the third most frequent cause of death for young people.

When we think about a depressed adult, we visualize someone who appears sad and forlorn. Some depressed children do look this way, but most look defiant, angry, or indifferent. One out of every six children in counseling is dealing with depression, yet these depressed children rarely describe themselves as feeling sad, overwhelmed, or defeated. The good news is that intervention makes a remarkable difference. Treatment has become increasingly effective as childhood depression is diagnosed earlier and treated with a variety of strategies that include both medication and counseling.

Why so much sadness? Life for many children has become riddled with stressful changes, a hurried routine, family strife, and violence. Children in the United States feel increasingly sad, angry, and futureless. Statistics about children show alarming increases in self-destructive behavior. These frightening facts include:

- One million adolescent girls (1 in 10) become pregnant yearly.

- Forty percent of high school seniors report getting drunk weekly.

- Alcohol-related accidents are the leading cause of teen deaths.

- Suicide rates for teens have doubled since 1968.

- Between 10 and 20% of teens attempt suicide.

- Homicide is the leading killer of minority youths.

- Thirty times more children are arrested today than were arrested in 1950.

Parents are increasingly less available to children. Fifty percent are divorced, and in most families, both parents are working at least one job. Children see and experience more trauma and abuse. They watch more television, usually alone, waiting for parents to return from work. School failure continues to increase. After-school recreational opportunities for kids are decreasing because of safety concerns or because transportation is unavailable. All these factors contribute to the stress level of children's lives and to their feelings of failure, isolation, and depression.

The onset of depression can be gradual or sudden; its duration can be brief or chronic. It can be associated with other disorders, especially anxiety, eating disorders, attention deficit disorder (ADHD), learning disability (LD), school failure, conduct disorders, and substance abuse. Short-term depression can be a normal response to a major loss, such as a divorce or death in the family, or the loss of friendships because of a family move. However, unresolved or chronic depression interferes with attention, motivation, and energy and soon affects every aspect of a child's life.

Depression is a "whole-body" emotional disorder. Besides mood changes, depression also involves changes in sleep, appetite, energy, general health, ability to concentrate and learn, and ability to control social behaviors. Angry outbursts cause tension at home and alienation at school. Complications of serious antisocial and delinquent behavior can develop while school performance decreases. Behavioral acting-out often involves drugs, alcohol, and sex, and suicidal thinking may develop.

ASSESSMENT

A diagnosis of depression needs to be considered when:

- a child shows a sudden change in mood or behavior
- behavioral extremes are evident—the child is either sad and withdrawn or angry and aggressive
- at school, a student has trouble concentrating or completing assignments, looks tired or sleepy, and often complains of stomach pains or headaches
- at home, a child is irritable, moody, or negative and becomes emotionally unavailable by withdrawing into the cloister of his or her room, music, or telephone
- sleeping and eating habits shift to either extreme.

Diagnostic Criteria

The parents' first complaint often concerns the constant tension and turmoil caused by their child's irritability; sullen attitude; or angry, defiant behavior. Three types of depression are recognized in the *DSM*. Depression is diagnosed the same for children as adults with consideration given to developmental age.

Major depression. For diagnosis, five of these ten symptoms must be apparent and must include either number one or number two:

1. The child experiences a depressed mood, meaning that he or she feels sad, unliked, and lonely; easily frustrated and generally irritable; or angry and negative (feelings that may make him or her want to argue and pick fights).

2. The child may also experience mood swings. If the child has diurnal mood variation there is a predictable up-down mood swing each day.

3. The child has little or no ability to derive pleasure from activities that he or she once enjoyed.

4. The child experiences appetite changes and loses or gains weight. Carbohydrate cravings are common in children with seasonal affective disorder (SAD, described below).

5. The child has changes in sleep patterns. He or she may sleep all the time yet never feel rested or may be unable to sleep. The child may be afraid to sleep alone because of nightmares. Adolescents can develop a reversed sleep-wake cycle.

6. The child's activity level changes. The child's movement is either excessive (fidgety) or so slow that he or she appears to be moving in slow motion.

7. The child always feels tired; even small tasks seem monumental.

8. The child feels like a failure, and afraid to try things; he or she may feel guilty or act apathetic.

9. The child has trouble concentrating and may be unable to make even a simple decision.

10. The child is preoccupied with thoughts about death and suicide.

Other symptoms include increased anxiety, excessive brooding and worrying, unreasonable fears and phobias, or feeling overwhelmed. Mood and anxiety disorders may exist simultaneously. With major depression, symptoms last for longer than two weeks. Psychotic features may occur. Auditory hallucinations are fairly common in younger children, who may describe hearing a voice that talks to them. Delusions are rare and indicate the possibility of bipolar disorder.

Seasonal Affective Disorder (SAD). SAD is a cyclic form of depression in which recurring episodes happen during the low-sunshine winter months. Children complain of fatigue, of being tired and sleepy, and of hunger, especially for starchy foods. This "mini-hibernation" is difficult to diagnose in children since the seasonal pattern takes several years to recognize.

Dysthymia. When sadness is not severe but does remain chronic, the disorder of dysthymia may be present. In children, the behavior that usually causes concern is negativity rather than sadness. Parents complain of their child being gloomy, angry, irritable, argumentative, tired, and often disobedient. The child is constantly frowning or complains or criticizes excessively. For diagnosis, symptoms must be apparent for at least a year, and no significant abatement can last longer than two months. Additionally, two of the following symptoms must exist:

- eating too little or too much

- sleeping too little or too much

- having chronic fatigue, low energy

- having low self-esteem

- experiencing poor concentration; difficulty deciding anything; little ability to follow through

- frequently feeling the future is hopeless

An important difference between dysthymia and major depression is that the child still finds pleasure in doing things. He or she still participates, likes to be with friends, and enjoys favorite activities. Dysthymia may be secondary to another disorder, especially ADHD, eating disorders, anxiety disorders, or several medical conditions such as rheumatoid arthritis. Dysthymia often begins in childhood and continues throughout one's life, developing into a depressive personality disorder.

Bipolar Disorder. The hallmark of this disorder is alternating episodes of low-energy depression and high-energy mania. In children, the high-energy, expansive mood of the mania cycle might show as irritability and explosive temper, especially when the child is frustrated. For diagnosis, the manic episode must show at least three of the following symptoms:

- Inflated self-esteem or exaggerated self-confidence. This symptom is often made evident by the child's taking on inappropriate responsibilities such as driving a car without a license, or by the child's challenging authority, arguing about limits, or defying rules.

- Decreased need for sleep without decreased energy.

- Rapid, pressured speech with little ability to stop and listen or irritable, argumentative complaining without ability to compromise.

- Flight of ideas—inability to sustain a train of thought.

- Excessive distractibility by either external or internal stimuli.

- Increased activity level at home, at school, and with friends. The child may throw himself or herself into a series of activities without completing any or may exhibit disorganized yet driven behavior.

- Compulsive people-seeking that can be very inappropriate, demonstrated by actions such as calling a friend during the night or speaking out during class.

- Impulsive behavior that is risky, dangerous, or socially inappropriate, and sometimes illegal. Borrowing the family car and taking friends for a fast ride down the interstate is a typical example of this behavior. This impulsivity can be aggravated by binge drinking or the use of illegal drugs.

- Sexual preoccupation that is inappropriate for developmental age. An example is an eight-year-old who calls "900" numbers.

The rapid and unpredictable shifts from manic to depressive states are confusing and frustrating to parents. During the manic state, a child does not recognize the inappropriateness of behavior or feelings. Emotional reactions to criticism or discipline are often extreme and unreasonable.

Bipolar illness is difficult to diagnose before adolescence. However, one-fourth of the children who experience major depression develop bipolar disorder. Those most at risk are those who are hyperactive, have temper outbursts and mood swings, and have a family history of bipolar disorder, major depression, or alcoholism. Children with major depression who are not at risk for developing bipolar disorder are those who are hypoactive or those who experience sadness and moodiness following an initial onset of depression that was sudden and began at a young age.

Assessment Tools

Multimodal assessment that addresses all aspects of the disorder is essential. It must include physical-medical assessment, intellectual-academic assessment, social-behavioral assessment, and an examination of family history and relationships. See Table 8.1 for a list of diagnostic tests.

Table 8.1 **Diagnostic Tests**

Rating Scales and Checklists	Interviews	Other Self-Report Tests
• Children's Depression Rating Scale, Revised	• Children's Assessment Scales (CAS)	• Children's Manifest Anxiety Scale
• The Bellevue Index of Depression (BID)	• Interview for the SADLI	• Minnesota Multiphasic Personality Inventory (for adolescents)
• Peer Nomination Index of Depression (PNID)	• Diagnostic Interview for Children and Adolescents (DICA)	• Milton Adolescent Personality Inventory
• School-age Depression Listed Inventory (SADLI)	• Diagnostic Interview Schedule for Children (DISC)	• Child Behavioral Screening Questionnaire
• Children's Depression Inventory (CDI)	• Interview Schedule for Children by Kovacs (ISC)	• Personality Inventory for Children (PIC)
• Short Children's Depression Inventory	• Kiddie SADS (K-SADS)	
• Beck Depression Inventory	• Behavior Inventory for Depressed Adolescents	
• Hamilton Depression Rating Scale (HDRES)		
• The Reynold's Adolescent Depression Scale		

Developmental Considerations

Infants, Toddlers and Preschoolers. Babies can become depressed. During the first year of life, depression may develop because of poor, disrupted, or abusive parenting. Depression can also be part of an attachment disorder that develops when an infant or a toddler loses a mother or primary caregiver because of the adult's death, illness, depression, addictions, or profound lack of parenting skills. This syndrome, called anaclitic depression, is characterized by delayed development, poor appetite or refusal to eat, apathy and withdrawal, low responsivity, and sleep disturbances. Most infants recover if normal parenting resumes within a few months. Without adequate caregiving, depression and/or attachment disorder can result in death, permanent developmental delays, or permanent disruption of emotional-behavioral development.

Depressed toddlers and preschoolers are often pouty and uncooperative. They may have excessive bouts of crying and throw temper tantrums. They may seek more adult attention than a child who is not depressed; separation anxiety is a typical symptom of depression. Sleeping and eating habits can be at either extreme. The child may appear sad or angry. He or she may withdraw from other children by hanging back and watching them and participate only to cause trouble by hitting, taking toys, or yelling. Most causes for depression at this young age are victimization through abuse or neglect; traumatic family events such as parental death; serious illness of a parent or sibling; or emotional or physical absence of a parent. Chronic depression during infancy and preschool years can:

- slow physical and cognitive growth
- delay acquisition of verbal skills
- interfere with academic learning
- decrease social competence and nonverbal communication
- result in permanent disability or death.

School-age children. Depression occurs in roughly 5 % of school-age children. Sad mood, low energy, irritability, poor self-esteem, and an inability to join in and have fun are common symptoms. School phobias may develop. Academic performance is almost always affected. Chronic complaints of physical aches and pains (head and stomach) are heard from 70% of depressed children. Enuresis (bedwetting) may develop. Behavioral acting-out often interferes with peer relationships. Hallucinations (hearing a voice talking to them) are described by a third of these children.

Depressed preteens are often described as sad, tired, and irritable. They have poor eye contact. Social withdrawal can become a significant problem. Suicidal thinking and talking may be covert except during explosive angry outbursts. Depression often affects the physical, emotional, academic, family, and social aspects of a preteen's life.

Adolescents. Adolescents who are seriously depressed have symptoms similar to those of younger children but have an increased degree of suicidal thinking, planning, and attempting. More girls suffer from major depression at this age (16%) than boys (10%). However, suicide attempts by boys are more often successful on the first try. Antisocial behaviors increase in both boys and girls and involve running away, stealing, shoplifting, sexual promiscuity, and abuse of drugs and alcohol. Some depressed teens may withdraw from both adults and peers, while others become obsessed with friends, even running away from home or ditching school to be with them.

Table 8.2 **Summary of Symptoms Depending on Child's Age**

Age	6-10 years	10-14 years	14-16 years
Incidence	5%	10%	Girls: 16% Boys: 10%
Symptoms	Enuresis, sadness, fatigue, irritability, behavioral acting out, verbal aggression, decline in academics, social withdrawal	Abnormal EEG, suicidal thinking and attempting, running away, stealing, drugs, sexual activity, inability to tolerate routine, restlessness, social hyperactivity or hypoactivity, sadness, fatigue, irritability, behavioral acting out, verbal aggression, decline in academics	

INTERVENTION STRATEGIES

What Counselors Can Do

Take a complete history. Ask about the following aspects of the child's life:

1. *Developmental.* Was the child's early history problematic, stressful, chaotic, or traumatic? Are there old problems or concerns?

2. *Physical-medical.* Request a full medical evaluation to rule out physical causes of the depression and to establish communication with the child's physician if medications are indicated. Are there any chronic medical conditions? Is the child taking any medications? Is there a history of depression or mood disorder? What are the child's physical complaints?

3. *Psychological.* Is there a family history of depression; a previous history of counseling; or known traumas for this child or for any member of the family?

4. *Academic-intellectual.* Is there any history of ADHD, LD, or school failure with the child or family? Has the child been successful in school? Have there been any sudden changes in achievement levels?

5. *Social-behavioral.* Does the child have friends? How do parents and teachers describe the child's ability to get along with others? What does the child report?

6. *Self-esteem.* How does the child describe strengths and problems? How positive or negative is the child's self-talk? What activities are listed as fun? What does the child feel he or she is "good at"? Remember that children typically underreport behavior and conduct problems.

7. *Family.* Ask about family history of such problems as mood disorders, phobias, alcoholism, and learning disabilities. (Often families have nonclinical labels for relatives who have chronic problems.) What is the relationship between the child's parents like? Interview the parents and child separately, the child first. Be sure the child understands that your counseling relationship with him or her is the primary, more important one.

Multimodal Treatment Strategies

Medical Strategies. Work with the child's physician to determine whether drug therapy (pharmacotherapy) is appropriate. Often medication provides the jump-start that is needed in treating depression. Help parents and the child understand how drugs work. Explain the risk of drug addiction, which is a typical concern of parents. Assure parents that medication does not turn their child into a drug addict. Explain what a trial schedule entails: a preliminary assessment is made before a drug treatment is tried for 8 to 12 weeks, and then a final assessment is made to determine effectiveness. During this time the child is monitored closely and is reassessed frequently. A child is not put on pills forever.

A combination of drug therapy and other strategies is often effective in treating depression. Most of the adult antidepressant drugs have been used with children with varying degrees of success. There are four primary classes of antidepressants:

1. *Tricyclic Antidepressants* (TCAs). Tricyclics (Tofranil, Norpromine, and Elavil) are less helpful in children than in adults. However, clinical use of tricyclics in depressed children who do not respond to nonpharmacological interventions appears warranted. Half of these youngsters do respond, if medication is continued for at least 8 to 10 weeks and other interventions are concurrent. Tricyclics especially can have serious side effects and should be prescribed and monitored by a psychiatrist or physician knowledgeable in pediatric psychopharmacology.

2. *Monoamine Oxidase Inhibitors (MAOIs).* MAOIs (Nardil and Parnate) are currently not used to treat depression in young adults. Side effects and overdosing are too risky.

3. *Selective Serotonin Reuptake Inhibitors (SSRIs).* SSRIs, such as Prozac, Zoloft, and Paxil, prevent the reuptake of the neurotransmitter serotonin. They have few serious side effects. Most important, they have effectively decreased depression in children and adolescents. SSRIs are also effective in treating childhood anxiety disorders as well as eating disorders. The combination of Prozac and Ritalin has been used successfully to treat the depressed adolescent.

4. *Lithium Carbonate (Li)*. Lithium has only recently been used to treat mood disorders in children. There is some evidence that lithium is effective for those youngsters who have bipolar disorder.

When medication is effective, there is marked improvement in ability to cope and to concentrate; to problem-solve about depression; and to communicate and cooperate with adults. The child's appetite and sleep needs are normalized (without extremes), emotional ups and downs are less overwhelming, and anxiety and irritability are decreased.

Physical strategies. Establish a physical activity program to increase the child's daily activity. Explain that exercise is a natural antidepressant. Take a baseline measure of how much "moving" and "getting outside" the child does daily. Solicit ideas from the child about how to increase this level by asking questions such as these: Which activities put you in a better mood? How does 'a better mood' feel different from a 'bad mood'? Make a contract with the child that outlines the changes he or she is willing to make. Set small goals, such as walking around the block once each day. Set up daily and weekly reinforcers, and teach self-reinforcement. Try to make the activities as enjoyable and fun as possible; this pleasure will increase the likelihood that the child will follow through. Does the child have a friend who will also participate? Ask the child whether he or she is willing to decrease time spent sitting each day. Discuss watching less TV and playing fewer video or computer games. Ideally, parents will cooperate, participate, and reinforce. For example, after supper, one parent can go for a walk or play a fun, noncompetitive sport with the child. (As part of each counseling session, consider walking for 15 minutes with the child.)

Cognitive Strategies. Depressed children think negatively. Their views of themselves, the world, and their future are negative and self-critical. Cognitive counseling methods include cognitive restructuring, attribution retraining, affective education with role-play, communication skills modeling, and social skills training.

During cognitive restructuring the counselor should:

- model for the child positive statements rather than negative
- ask the child to list one success each day
- have the child practice accepting compliments
- teach the connection between what people say, feel, and do
- teach self-monitoring of negative automatic thoughts and self-statements
- teach the child to identify and to modify dysfunctional beliefs
- train the child in positive assertiveness.

Depressed children tend to attribute their successes to others. Attribution retraining teaches, models, and practices with the child statements that reflect succeeding on his or her own rather than succeeding because of assistance from someone else. (*I did it and I did it well* rather than *I did okay because someone helped me, but I'll probably never be able to do it again on my own.*)

Affective education teaches children the language of feelings. Young children, and often older children, too, do not know the words to describe their internal feelings. Ask the child to identify his or her "inside feelings" and describe a recent situation that elicited good or bad—or light or dark—feelings. Employ facial expression charts and feelings games and books. These make effective parent-child homework assignments. Teach feeling words. Role-model and practice during the therapy session. Use fill-in-the-blank techniques, such as, I feel _____ when _____ happens. I can tell that other children (or parents) feel _____ when their face looks like _____ and they do _____.

Depressed children often mumble responses or avoid answering at all. What answers they do offer are often negative, sullen, or sarcastic. They seldom look directly at the person to whom they are speaking. Communication skills training teaches these children how and why to communicate more effectively. Communication skills training includes teaching:

- how to make and sustain eye contact

- sitting and standing tall and straight

- how to speak more loudly or more clearly

- how and why to answer a question with more than just one word

• how and why it is important to make polite ("small") talk

Behavioral social skills training provides depressed children with the social skills they sorely lack. Depressed children are often unable to make friends; they may even annoy or irritate peers because of their inability to read social cues. Social skills training includes teaching the child appropriate social behaviors, such as joining a group, making friends, negotiating disagreements with peers, and making apologies. Counselors can model and role-play how to:

• say hello

• invite another child to play

• ask to join in when kids are playing

• apologize

• ask for help

• give compliments

• take turns

• compromise

• follow rules

• increase self-control

• identify problem situations.

It is useful for a counselor to also role-play the inappropriate behavior, by acting negative, bossy, or critical, and then talk about how it feels and why it is not effective in eliciting positive responses from others.

Social skills training does not need to be complicated. Small counseling groups are an effective format to teach, to model, to practice, and to discuss what works and what doesn't work in getting along with friends. Playing simple games such as *Risk* or checkers is an excellent way to practice these skills. With the child's permission, demonstrate to the parents the specific social behaviors that are being practiced. Ask them to model and reinforce appropriate social behaviors at home.

Academic Strategies. Work with the teacher to establish a classroom program in which the child can be successful. If the child's academic record has been chronically poor or inconsistent, request a staff meeting to discuss initiating a learning disability evaluation, including an evaluation for ADHD. If depression is sudden and the child's grades have recently slipped, talk with the teacher about adjusting assignments so that the child can catch up and again be successful in school.

Let the parent know that the whole team—parent, child, teacher, and counselor—is working toward finding new ways to make school positive and successful. Ask the teacher for suggestions to make this goal attainable. Implement one suggestion at a time; begin with the one that has the best chance of success. Ask the teacher about the child's behavior and peer relationships. Again, ask assistance in setting small, specific goals to increase appropriate peer interactions. Perhaps the teacher can find ways to pair the depressed child with an outgoing child during cooperative tasks.

Family Strategies. Assess the emotional health of the family. Encourage parents to focus on any of their own personal problems or marital problems. Be realistic with the child about the family situation. Be especially careful to listen for the child's feeling responsible for creating and correcting adult issues; correct any self-blame or guilt. If possible, engage the family in short-term family therapy to support and to reinforce the new skills the child is learning, to encourage positive communication, to teach positive reinforcement, and to address relevant family issues. Almost all children are poor at self-monitoring, so maintaining behavioral programs and family changes needs to be the parents' responsibility.

What Parents Can Do

Teach parents the importance of spending positive one-on-one time with their child; ask them to keep a log so that you can assess the amount of this time. Suggest ways that parents can spend pleasant time together, for example, cooking a meal, taking a walk together, or playing cards. Identify regular times when the family will curtail all distractions and eat a meal together.

Teach parents to use positive statements with their child. Have parents keep a verbatim written record (for example, on a piece of paper taped to the refrigerator) of each positive statement they make to their child. Encourage this to become a cooperative family effort. Teach both the parents and the child that in general, people are treated as they treat others. Urge parents to be generous with verbal and secondary reinforcers.

Teach parents to listen to their child. Model active listening—listening with full attention without interrupting, arguing, criticizing, or offering a solution. Stress the importance of not letting anything interrupt time with a child, including phone calls. Suggest effective communication strategies such as these:

- Be brief with directions, requests, and compliments.

- Be direct. (Say the behavior that you want in one positive sentence, for example, "Please talk, don't whine, and I'll listen.")

- Make "I" statements rather than accusatory "you" statements, for example, "I can't understand when you mumble and don't look at me."

- Urge parents to reserve some weekend time for fun activities. Help the parents identify family, friends, or organizations that can help. Encourage friendships and identify times when the child could include a friend.

- Advise parents to limit the child's phone time, TV time, and even time alone in his or her bedroom. Help the parents and child agree on rules and limits.

Persuade parents to limit the amount of time the child spends home alone and/or the time spent home alone baby-sitting siblings. Help parents find supervised after-school fun activities for the child and, if necessary, ways to solve transportation problems.

Encourage parents to establish a routine that includes doing regular physical activities with the child. These activities can be short and simple but need to be fun, such as walking to the store for an ice cream treat or making cookies together.

Help parents identify the stressful times in the daily routine, such as mornings and suppertime. Many depressed kids are at their worst in the morning and late afternoon. Help parents uncover ways to reduce conflicts during these times.

Depressed children are unusually antagonistic with their siblings.

Explore with the parents ways to give each child space from the others. During therapy, model a family meeting that allows each family member to speak out and to list concerns, worries, and wishes. Help the family make a list of goals.

Remind parents that as the adults, they need to assume responsibility for follow-through; children are poor at remembering new responsibilities.

Model cognitive restructuring. Teach parents how to make positive, noncritical statements to their child.

Encourage parents to educate themselves about depression. Help them to understand that depression is a physical, neurological, emotional, and behavioral disorder and that outside help is important and effective.

If the parents are also depressed or struggling with a major problem, such as alcoholism or the marital relationship, encourage them to begin their own counseling. Their own healing will help their child.

What Teachers Can Do

Children with social problems find school painful and unpleasant. If they also have trouble learning, they will have difficulty relating to the teachers. It is likely that a depressed child is alienated from the teacher, as well as from peers, through behavior and attitude. Also, the teacher and parents may be at odds with each other since both are frustrated with the child. As a counselor, your first task is to assure a teacher that you are not interfering or casting blame, and that you are not telling the teacher how to teach. Keep in mind that the teacher is responsible for over 20 children at the same time, all day, five days a week.

Ask the teacher to describe concerns, observations, and frustrations about this student. Listen to what is observed as problematic behaviors of the child. Ask the teacher whether the child exhibits the typical signs of depression—signs that may at first look more like conduct disorder. Does the child complain of headaches and stomachaches? Does he or she have a low frustration tolerance? Is he irritable? Does he or she appear lethargic or apathetic? Ask whether there has been a midyear slump, or whether the child's behavior changed suddenly, symptoms that could indicate SAD. Also ask questions about friendships, such as: Does the child have friends? Are the friendships positive and healthy? Is the child isolated from others? Do other children complain about the child's behavior? Is this child chosen by others to participate in group activities and playground games?

Ask the teacher how you can help and identify behaviors you could work on during therapy sessions. Review the types of intervention strategies you are using in therapy and those that the parents are trying at home. Discuss simple cognitive restructuring strategies, social modeling, and specific positive comments that can be used in a natural way in the classroom. Share information about the dynamics of depression.

ANTICIPATED PROGRESS AND OUTCOMES

An effective treatment strategy should show positive results within six to eight weeks. Any of the checklist assessments given before and during treatment will evaluate treatment effectiveness and reinforce positive changes.

Studies of depression in children have only recently started to include long-term follow-up studies. So far, studies show that the average duration of a major depressive disorder is six to eight months. Of the cases studied, 40% went into remission within six months and 90% did so within 18 months. Younger children had longer episodes than older children did. Within five years following the first depressive episode, there was a 70% risk of a second episode, which usually occurred during the first two years. Risk of recurrence was greater if an underlying dysthymic disorder was also present. The average duration of dysthymic disorder was three years. For most children, the time from diagnosis to full recovery is six to seven years. During this long period of time, many aspects of a child's life, such as self-attitude, academics, and social skills, are compromised.

Untreated major depression can be deadly. Even if suicide is avoided, chronic depression disrupts development. Depression interferes with learning social, language, and academic skills. It is the lack of social skills—the inability to make and to maintain friendships—which makes it hard to like oneself or to enjoy life. This disruption in development can have permanent effects. The good news is that treatment is usually effective once the behavior and emotional problems are recognized as depression and the depression is treated.

RESOURCES
Books for Parents, Teachers, and Counselors

Dubuque, S. *A Parent's Survival Guide to Childhood Depression.* Plainview, NY: Childswork/Childsplay, 1992.

Describes how Nicholas and his family learn to cope with Nicholas' depression. Includes a useful resource guide for parents.

Goldberg, I. *Questions and Answers About Depression and Its Treatment.* Philadelphia, PA: The Charles Press, 1993.

Describes depression, symptoms, and treatment options.

Ingersoll, B., and S. Goldstein. *Lonely, Sad, and Angry: Parent's Guide to Depression and Adolescence.* New York, NY: Doubleday, 1995.

For parents and counselors. Describes assessment, symptoms, causes, treatment, and medications.

March, J., ed. *Anxiety Disorders in Children and Adolescents.* New York, NY: Guilford Press, 1996.

Comprehensive guide to understanding, diagnosing, and treating anxiety disorders in children. Recommended for counselors.

Nowicki, S., and M. Duke. *Helping the Child Who Doesn't Fit In.* Atlanta, GA: Peachtree, 1992.

Describes why some children are social misfits and provides a guide to teachable skills. (Some children are depressed or become depressed because of the daily rejection.)

Pipher, M. *Reviving Ophelia: Saving the Selves of Adolescent Girls.* New York, NY: Bantam, 1995.

Addresses the issues that challenge adolescent girls. Extremely well written and includes many case studies. For counselors, teachers, and parents.

Reynolds, W., and H. Johnson. *Handbook of Depression in Children and Adolescents.* New York, NY: Plenum, 1990.

Written for the professional. Covers the basics of depression and its treatment for children and adolescents.

Shapiro, P. *A Parent's Guide to Childhood Depression.* New York, NY: Dell, 1994.

One of a series from the Children's Hospital of Philadelphia. Includes treatment, medications, and resources. For parents and counselors.

Books for Children

Adderholt-Eliot, M. *Perfectionism: What's Bad About Being Good.* Minneapolis, MN: Free Spirit Press, 1995.

Challenges perfectionism and discusses depressed children's tendency toward negative self-talk and unrealistic expectations.

Dambrower, J. *Getting To Know Your Feelings.* Charlotte, NC: KIDRIGHTS, 1995.

Teaches how to explain emotions to young children and includes an audiotape of sing-along songs.

Dubuque, N., and S. Dubuque. *Kid Power Tactics for Dealing with Depression.* Plainview, NY: Childswork/Childsplay, 1992.

Eleven-year-old Nicholas gives helpful information on depression and details 15 "kid power" tactics to help children cope.

Hipp, E. *Fighting Invisible Tigers: A Stress Management Guide for Teens.* Minneapolis, MN: Free Spirit Press, 1996.

Helpful for the depressed middle school and teenage child.

Perino, J. *I Think I'm Hopeless. . . But I Could Be Wrong.* Charlotte, NC: KIDRIGHTS, 1996.

Written for the older child, the author explores faulty thinking and describes how to change those patterns.

Simon, N. *How Do I Feel?* Chicago, IL: A. Whitman Publisher, 1970.
A touching picturebook in which a young boy describes all the different kinds of feelings he experiences in the course of one day.

Agencies and Organizations

KIDRIGHTS
8902 Otis Avenue
Indianapolis, IN 46216
(800) 892-KIDS

Distributor of videos that address depression and other life problems of children.

Free Spirit Press
400 First Ave. North, Suite 616
Minneapolis, MN 55401-1730
(800) 735-7323

This press specializes in learning materials for parents, teachers, and children. Publishes books on building self-esteem, health, and coping strategies. Catalog available.

National Association for Mental Health
1021 Prince St.
Alexandria, VA 22314-2971

American Psychiatric Association
1400 K Street, N.W.
Washington, D.C. 20005
(202) 682-6000

Provides information on state and local chapters.

American Psychological Association

750 First st.
Washington, D.C. 20002-4242
(202) 336-5500

Provides information on state and local chapters.

National Foundation for Depressive Illness
(800) 248-4344

National Depressive and Manic Depressive Association
(800) 826-3632

CHAPTER 9
Traumatized Children

The therapist listened as Julie chose her words carefully.

"My husband Jack never hit my kids. . . but he did hit me. During these awful fights David and Bruce, my sons, would pull at Jack's legs and beg him to stop. They were just little boys then."

Julie stopped talking and looked right at her therapist.

"They still got hurt, didn't they?" she asked. "They got hurt by watching him do that to me."

Children experience trauma in two basic ways—as a result of a single isolated event, such as a car accident, or as a result of a series of painful events such as physical or verbal abuse within the family.

American children are living in a dangerous world. Car accidents and guns kill more young people than any illness. A recent study by the Johns Hopkins School of Public Health documented that 37% of childhood fatalities are caused by automobile accidents, and 27% are caused by gunshot wounds.

Physical, sexual, and emotional abuse as well as physical and emotional neglect traumatize children and affect their psychological and physical development. When mistreatment happens repeatedly within a family, the physical and psychological damage to children can be extensive and long-lasting. Sexual abuse crosses physical and emotional boundaries. Incest is often a secret abuse perpetrated with confusing messages; it causes severe trauma to children. Statistics describing the number of children injured or killed by abuse are sad and alarming. There are 300,000 documented physical abuse cases per year; 5,000 to 6,000 documented deaths from abuse per year; and 500,000 documented sexual abuse cases per year.

Witnessing abuse and violence is also harmful and traumatic. Only recently have mental health clinicians and researchers begun to observe and track young clients who witness violence between parents or from a parent to a sibling. Initial reports estimate that 3 to 10 million children are emotionally at risk because of witnessing violence within the home. When a child witnesses his parent or sibling getting hurt, he experiences terror, insecurity and rage. Traumatized children are terrified that they will get hurt or that their parent or sibling will get hurt again. (This fear is well founded. It is estimated that 30 to 40% of children with battered mothers are also battered, either physically or sexually.) These children are fearful of living in a hurtful, unpredictable environment. They also feel rage at the assailant, at the victim for not protecting himself or herself, and at themselves for not preventing or stopping the violence.

Witnessing violence outside the family but within the community or school also traumatizes children. In some parts of our cities, children witness violent acts such as drive-by shootings, fire-bombings, suicides, or robberies with gunfire. In 1995, 91% of the children in New Orleans and 72% in Washington, D.C., had observed neighborhood violence; 40% of junior high students in New Haven, Connecticut, had seen a stabbing or a shooting; 10% of grade school children in Boston had observed violent crimes.

Another alarming trend is the portrayal of violence as humorous and without realistic consequences on TV shows, on videos, and in movies. Research now shows that children who watch TV for long hours are learning to behave aggressively and harmfully and may be desensitized to the effects of violence.

Brain activity changes following abuse. A traumatic event triggers a prolonged alarm reaction. The acute response is a release of neurotransmitters that arouse and activate the body. Heart rate accelerates, breathing becomes rapid, muscles tense, and blood pressure rises. These reactions may persist for a long time. While children who survived the Waco fire were undergoing medical treatment, the staff observed that the children's sleeping heart rates remained abnormally high for weeks.

It appears that the more unpredictable the trauma, the more violent the event, and the more chronic the situation, the more damaging the impact on the child. If the external world is chaotic, violent and frightening, the brains of abused and neglected children will develop and organize to prepare for chaos, violence, and fear. According to Dr. Bruce Perry at the 1995 Rosenberry Conference in Denver, Colorado, "Traumatized children. . . will often, at baseline, be in a fearful state of hyperarousal."

The more threatened the child feels, the more primitive his or her style of thinking. When a traumatized child simply thinks about past trauma, he or she becomes anxious and afraid and is less able to concentrate, to think clearly, to control emotions, and to behave in a reasonable, age-appropriate way. The traumatized child pays close attention to adults' body posture and tone of voice and scans the environment for potential threats. Thus, it is essential for the therapist to keep the counseling experience as nonthreatening as possible. This may mean not leaning too close to the child, not moving suddenly, and not touching the child.

ASSESSMENT
Diagnostic Criteria

Clinically, it is important to assess whether a child's life is disrupted totally (meaning that trauma affects play, school, and family life) or only during certain activities and in specific environments. If a child experiences any of the following symptoms for over six months, then the diagnosis of Post-traumatic Stress Disorder (PTSD) is appropriate.

- The child has experienced or witnessed an event involving death or serious injury or the threat or possibility of death or serious injury. The child shows an emotional response of intense fear, helplessness, or horror. The child's behavior may be disorganized, regressed, violent, or agitated.

- The child's behavior or thinking is disrupted because of reexperiencing. Reexperiencing is evident in any of these ways: Recurrent and intrusive recollections of the traumatic event in images, thoughts, or perceptions; recurrent nightmares of the event; and behavioral reenactments of the event, in play or with peers.

- Intense distress from internal or external cues that resemble the traumatic event. This can include retelling, hearing, or even thinking about the event.

- Physiological alarm state triggered from exposure to external or internal cues. The heart rate increases, breathing becomes rapid, and the body prepares for danger.

- The child shows persistent avoidance of specific stimuli, including denial and/or numbing. There are frequent efforts to avoid thoughts, feelings, or conversations about the trauma and consistent efforts to avoid activities, places, or people connected to the trauma. There is an inability to recall important details and interest or participation in normal activities is diminished. Finally, there is a feeling of detachment from others.

- The range of expressed emotions is restricted.

- The child feels "futureless" and has difficulty talking about hopes and plans.

- The child is troubled by persistent symptoms of increased arousal. Symptoms include an inability to fall asleep or stay asleep; outbursts of anger or periods of irritability (which cause peers and adults to feel uncomfortable); poor concentration and memory during school; chronic hypervigilance; and an increased startle response.

A child's response to a traumatic event changes if the trauma is repeated. In 1996, Perry reported that repeated trauma increases the chance of internalizing a dysfunctional pattern of alarm state in the brain. With repeated trauma, recall becomes blurred, fragmented, or inaccurate because defense mechanisms (disassociation, numbing, and denial) prevent remembering. Also, if trauma involves parental abuse, the emotional and behavioral states are more intense and often beyond the child's control.

The child who is experiencing PTSD may appear anxious, hyperactive, agitated, or restless or may appear withdrawn and have symptoms of depression. The traumatized child may appear to be daydreaming for long periods of time or may be secretive and engaged in solitary, repetitive pretend games. He or she may be tired because of trouble sleeping or be frightened by nightmares. The child may also exhibit angry outbursts or temper tantrums.

Issues to Explore

Reports. Referring agencies or professionals usually have written reports describing the traumatic event. Request reports from police, social services, or medical professionals to get an objective account of what happened.

Interviews. Before meeting with the child, first talk to a parent or a reliable adult about the trauma and the child's responses. Obtain information about the child's life and the triggering events from all available sources so that the child doesn't have to talk about the trauma too early in therapy. Remember that talking about the trauma can trigger an overwhelming alarm reaction in the child. Interview the parent/adult and ask:

What is the child's attachment history?
Has the parent been a reliable and safe caretaker?
What was the child's temperament before the trauma? Has it changed?
What was the child's coping style? Has it changed?
What is the child's present coping style?
Does the child's behavior reflect repetitive reenactment in play, conversations, or nightmares?
What is the child's history of traumatic events?
What is the nature, frequency, and duration of the events?
What are all the present major stressors? Ask about such changes as divorce or remarriage of parents, imprisonment of a parent, out-of-home placement, and geographic or school changes.
What is the family's coping style for stress?

Interview the child, but remember not to "retraumatize." Memory of the event may be unclear or inaccessible. Remember that when a child describes a traumatic memory, the sequence of the events may be mixed up, but the crucial details will be present. If the trauma was repeated or chronic, memory may be possible. Conversely, when the trauma was a single episode, the memory may be repeated over and over when the child wants to stop remembering. Memory can be a clue to whether the event happened once or many times.

Children exposed to trauma often see their future foreshortened, limited, or nonexistent. They lose a belief in a limitless future and believe they will die before growing up. Ask a child to predict and describe what he or she will be doing next year or as a grown up.

Time is distorted during a traumatic event; it is both lengthened and shortened. When frightened, children will often count to themselves to distance the fear. They may sing songs or repeat a prayer. Ask the child what he or she did during the trauma. Sometimes when children mix up the sequence of events they alter time to include a warning sign, a predictor. This predictor functions as an "omen" to give the child the illusion of control. For example, a child may feel that if he or she had only paid attention to the predictor, the terrible event could have been avoided. Ask the child to try to remember any warning or omen. Check on the reality of this perception. Remember that the omen will now function to elicit fear and alarm. Fear is a strong emotional current in all traumatized children and strongly inhibits them from disclosing what has happened. Traumatized children experience:

- fear of what will happen next
- fear of the perpetrator
- fear of being blamed
- fear of not being believed
- fear of losing family
- fear of losing more power and control.

Children repeat the themes of the traumatic event in their dreams, their play, and their acting-out behavior. For example, five-year-old Andrea was molested by a daycare provider, a self-proclaimed witch. Over and over Andrea would play with a pretend witch who would appear and invade the sand tray, the dollhouse, or a puppet show. As Andrea began healing, she was able to control the witch, to throw her out, to beat her up—to take control.

Children who have experienced sexual abuse become developmentally inappropriately sexualized. They are left with overwhelming premature sexual knowledge and awareness. One way the child copes is to reenact what has happened through sexualized play on dolls, on themselves, and with other children. If a child is displaying inappropriate sex play, the child has learned this behavior through exposure or experience. Examples of sexualized behavior may include preoccupation with sexual talk and actions, masturbation, sexual activity appropriate only for adults, and/or sexual victimization of self or others. For example, five-year-old Joshua, who had been molested by a neighbor, mimicked anal intercourse with other children. Ask the caretaking adult about a child's nightmares, play themes, and behavior changes—especially behavior with peers.

In summary, it is necessary to obtain the following information from reports and interviews:

- nature of the trauma
- degree of the threat
- single versus repeated trauma
- availability of support
- sense of control, both unrealistic (omens) or realistic
- timing of the intervention (the earlier the intervention, the more likely a child will heal).

Behavior Inventories. The following behavior inventories are useful for evaluating children who have experienced trauma:

- Dean Behavior Checklist for Child and Adolescent
- Children's Garden Attachment Model
- Reynolds Child Mood Inventory
- Children's Impact of Traumatic Events (CITIES)
- Child Disassociative Checklist
- Child Sexual Behavior Inventory, Version 1.

Projective Techniques. These projective techniques are effective for assessment of trauma in children:

- HOUSE-TREE-PERSON. Described in the "Divorce" chapter of this book.

- Self-Portrait. Children who have been traumatized often distort the parts that were hurt. A child who was forced to engage in oral sex might omit a mouth on a drawing or, more likely, draw it huge, open, and bright red in color. Sometimes children leave off parts of their body or draw more primitively than is usual for their age group.

- Rosebush Drawing. Described in the "Divorce" chapter.

Developmental Considerations

There is an ongoing debate about the age at which a child is most vulnerable to trauma. Studies by Perry (1995) revealed that the younger child has fewer coping skills, less language, and, most importantly, an immature nervous system. Clearly what changes with age is how children express emotional pain, as does the understanding of why awful things happen.

Children under six will regress; for example, a five-year-old will wet the bed, use baby talk, throw intense temper tantrums, or cling to a safe parent. These young children have less language to describe the event and to ask questions and will act out the trauma with behavior. They will often have distortions in memory except for the core experience of the trauma. Because their cognitive abilities are still pre-operational, they have illogical cause-and-effect understanding; they will often blame themselves for events over which they have no control. Children younger than six cannot understand an event from another's perspective; they can focus on only one emotion at a time, and they may become sexualized from sexual abuse.

School-age children will display disorganized behavior even if they are able to express in words what happened to them. They have more mature thought processes, and their thinking is more logical, less egocentric, and less concrete; they can conceptualize several emotions simultaneously. They can use language to ask questions and to make sense of and to gain control over the experience. They will have valid questions about why this traumatic event happened to them and will question possible motives. At age 9 or 10, these children are able to shift from assigning an external, simplistic explanation for what happened to an internal and more psychological explanation. School-age children show gender differences in their acting-out behaviors. Girls display more disassociative behavior and retreat into a private, fantasy world. Boys often become aggressive.

Trauma experienced in the first two years of life carries an enormous risk; it can interrupt or damage the attachment process. During the first few years, a child is building an internal model of the world based on the relationship with and caretaking of the parent. The securely attached child is able to develop a strong, independent sense of self. Children growing up in neglectful, inconsistent, or violent families experience an insecure, inconsistent attachment. They learn not to trust. The long-term studies of these children show a tremendous negative impact on learning, social relationships, and behavior. If there has been strong early attachment, healing from a traumatic event is much more likely to occur, so it is vital to assess the strength of trust and attachment.

Trauma experienced by the young child also disrupts memory. Studies have documented that three-to-six-year-old children are more vulnerable to misleading suggestions following trauma. All children tend to minimize and underreport abuse. Younger children minimize even more because of language limitation, memory disruption, and fear of consequences. The older child may underreport because of self-blame, shame, conflicting loyalties, and fear.

Traumagenic States of Children

Another part of assessment and treatment planning is identifying the emotional states created by trauma. Not all children will experience all of these emotional states, but the following is a framework based on Beverly James' work, *Treating Traumatized Children,* which allows counselors to evaluate a traumatized child, to set treatment goals, to plan appropriate strategies, and to mark progress.

1. *Self-blame.* Most children blame themselves for the bad thing that happened. They then begin to believe they are bad and begin to feel guilt and shame. It is crucial for the therapist to uncover this self-blaming belief system.

2. *Powerlessness.* Part of all traumas is the experience of powerlessness. The therapist's task is to help the child resolve and change this acquired state of being a powerless victim. Without intervention, some children continue to play the role of the victim in order to gain attention and protection; other children turn helplessness into aggression and look for other chil-

dren to victimize.

3. *Loss and betrayal.* Within each experience of trauma is an experience of betrayal and loss—loss of trust, innocence, freedom, and confidence. This experience of loss disrupts the foundation of trust that is basic to learning to relate to others. Grieving is essential. If the traumatized child does not grieve, anger and sadness become negativity. This negativity turned outward becomes aggression; turned inward it becomes depression.

4. *Fragmentation of body experience.* Memory storage is state-dependent. A specific odor, a type of adult, or a specific room can trigger an intense reliving of the traumatic event and elicit an overwhelming panic response. The therapist needs to do body work so that the child can relearn to trust his or her own strength and body and to integrate the experience. Mastery needs to include physical successes, such as outdoor challenges (a climbing wall or ropes course), dance, sports, or self-defense classes.

5. *Post-traumatic play.* Children's reenactment of the event may appear mechanistic, ritualistic, secretive, and without pleasure. The therapist provides a safe place for the child to play and helps the child to gradually change the "story" to include ways the child can be safe and powerful.

6. *Stigmatization.* Children who have been traumatized feel different and isolated from their peers. Shame and alienation can develop. Group work in school or in therapy with peers can help decrease the feelings of being different.

7. *Destructiveness.* Some children become violent, aggressive, or sexualized and hurt others or themselves. Revenge and power are the goals. This dangerous behavior needs to be confronted and brought under control before healing can occur. (Some children hide their destructive behaviors.) The therapist and parents need to teach, model, and practice safe ways of showing anger.

8. *Sexualization and eroticization.* Inappropriate sexual behavior is often the clue that leads to identification of sexual abuse. A child may have experienced an incomprehensible mixture of power, rewards, attention, threats, shame, guilt, and pain while being sexually exploited. A therapist needs to

slowly untangle both the memories of the experience as well as the child's understanding of it, and teach appropriate sexual boundaries.

9. *Dissociation.* One way a child survives overwhelming terror is to remove himself or herself, psychologically or emotionally, from the experience. The therapist needs to evaluate the degree of dissociation.

10. *Attachment disorders.* Secure attachment develops when the responsive parent provides a secure, safe, predictable environment. Children with secure attachments learn that the world is a positive place and that they are valued. Impaired attachment occurs with repeated neglect and abusive treatment, particularly when abuse occurs in the early years. There is no guaranteed way to protect a child from trauma, but a strong, healthy attachment to a responsible, nurturing adult allows healing.

INTERVENTION STRATEGIES
What Counselors Can Do

Turn down the alarm state. Remember that the traumatized child is in a constant state of low-level fear. Early sessions should focus on teaching the child and caretaker how to quiet the alarm state. Relaxation techniques to help calm the child may be useful. One useful relaxation tool is visualization. First, create a place for the child to sit in a relaxed, comfortable position. Provide cuddly stuffed animals and play soft music. Ask the child to close his or her eyes but don't force it. (At first, the child will probably be too fearful, but children can imagine and visualize very well with their eyes open.) The goal is to have the child imagine a safe place. Most children are attracted to the image of a private garden. Ask the child to think about what this place is like while you remind him or her of the senses of touch, sight, sound, smell, temperature, and texture. Ask the child to think about how pleasant this place is and to focus on feelings of relaxation, safety, and calm. Add a worry tree upon which the child can leave his or her worries. Another image to add could be a protector, a guardian angel, or a guide who will keep the child safe. To reinforce the image of a safe place, ask the child to draw what was imagined. This picture can be taken home and hung above his bed or be kept in a private place.

Ask what the family is already doing to relax at home, and encourage them to continue or begin predictable, consistent routines. Encourage the family to have a bedtime ritual, such as a bath followed by reading a story, doing visualization, or listening to soft music. Teach both the parents and the child other relaxation techniques such as rhythmic breathing and progressive muscle relaxation. To teach rhythmic breathing, if the child is comfortable and not afraid, ask him or her to lie down with a pillow under the head, knees bent, and feet solid on the floor. Guide the child by asking him or her to breathe in through the nose while you count to three and then breathe out through the mouth for another count of three. Progressive muscle relaxation entails having the child (and parents) tighten and relax each group of muscles. Again, first determine that the child is not too fearful, and then ask the child to lie down, eyes closed and palms up. Guide the child gently through the tightening and relaxing of each muscle group, beginning with the toes and feet and ending with the neck and face.

Address nightmares. Almost all traumatized children struggle with frightening nightmares and sleep difficulties. The first step is to help the child talk about bad dreams. Some children will communicate nonverbally through sand tray work, dollhouse play, or puppet stories that recreate the dream. Other children choose to draw the frightening parts of the dream. Any of these communication methods that occur in a safe place with safe adults listening will diminish the fears. The dream usually represents some part of the trauma, often without symbolism and with the perpetrators just as they are. For example, after five-year-old Anna was molested by her adolescent male cousin, she began dreaming nightly about the cousin chasing her. She'd wake up crying and would need to sleep with her parents. As Anna told and retold her nightmare with both words and sand tray work, the nightmare became an effective resource for healing. The therapist continued working with Anna and her parents to help her regain a sense of power and mastery over her trauma. Anna and her father decided to make a magic wand to use in the dream. Anna decided she would have her dog and both parents "placed" in her dream. She created her own magic words, which were simple and to the point: "Go away!" During therapy, she practiced using the words and visualizing her new dream. At home, she practiced with her parents. When Anna asked whether her real dog could sleep in her room, her parents agreed that it was a good idea. A nightlight was put in her room, and soft music became part of the bedtime ritual. These tactics helped Anna increase her sense of confidence, power, and control over her trauma and fears.

Manage intense emotional states. Traumatized children, especially those who have been abused, have difficulty modulating intense emotions. The alarm state—hypervigilance and readiness for threat—is easily activated. New theories about trauma victims describe an alteration of brain development that results in an overfunctioning of the primitive brain and an underdevelopment of the thinking, rational brain.

The child's rage is one of the most difficult emotions for both the child and for the caretaking adults. Talk with the parents about anger, and ask them about rage outbursts. Ask the parents to note the triggers and the response of the family to these outbursts, and to track the timing of the outburst. The child is angry with the perpetrator, angry with the parents either for not protecting him or her or for being a perpetrator, and angry at his or her own powerlessness. This anger may be displaced onto a target that the child feels is safer, such as police, social services, doctors, or the therapist.

One goal of therapy is to allow the anger to be vented safely and, if possible, appropriately, even if the targeted person is not the one who caused the trauma. Don't argue with the child about the rationality of either the anger or the target of the anger. Safe expression of anger is what is important. Assign homework to the adult and child during this phase, so that they can practice anger expression daily. However, be sure there is a consistent message from all adults about the rules for anger expression, such as it is not okay to hurt yourself or others or to damage anyone's property.

Let's return to the example. Little Anna began to have bloody dreams in which she stabbed the boy who molested her. In one session, Anna and her therapist practiced anger using paper tearing. Anna tore sheet after sheet. After she finished, sweaty yet smiling, she had filled five large garbage bags with paper and asked, "Can we save this for my mother and father?" The therapist presented the garbage bags to Anna's parents and then discussed ways for Anna and her parents to practice venting her anger each day at home. The therapist also discussed with Anna and her parents different warning behaviors that show that anger or fear needs to be "let out." In addition, the parents practiced expressing their own anger about the molestation.

Teach containment. One priority for the counselor is to teach children how to leave their emotional work in the therapy room—the skill of containment. You can teach children containment with concrete tools such as a shoebox, a folder, or a notebook. The child puts all the drawings, letters, and other "work" in a container and leaves the container in the therapy room. Near the end of each session, have a closing ritual such as blowing out a candle and making a wish. Then talk about what the child is doing for fun after the session. Tell that child that he or she is free to play, to be with friends, or to return to school without having scary memories interfere. Sometimes it is helpful to do something physical at the end of the session, such as stretching, playing music, or shaking out all the tension in the muscles plus shaking out all the "hurts in the heart." Suggest that parents not ask the child about the session after it is over; instead, they should plan something to do together after each visit to the counselor.

Do boundary work. Children who have endured trauma have had their personal boundaries broken, both physically and emotionally. The first task is to reteach them what a personal boundary is. To a concrete thinker (all young children), a boundary can be explained using skin as an example. Children can see, touch, and feel how their skin keeps them separate from others. Also teach about ways boundares are entered by touching, and that touching can be good, bad, or neutral.

School-age children can begin to understand a psychological boundary. Practice what is a comfortable distance for different relationships—for example, for family members, for friends, and for teachers. Use yarn to have a child create a visual boundary. Pay attention to how well a child creates the personal space desired. To model appropriate behaviors, always ask permission about such things as sitting close and hugging. Also model and practice saying "no" or moving away when someone infringes on your boundary.

Make sense of the trauma. At the beginning of the treatment process, explain that counseling will help the child make sense of what has happened. In *Treating Traumatized Children,* Beverly James uses these words to explain the counseling process to a child:

> We'll do this work when you're ready. It will be kind of like driving a car together or flying a plane as pilot and copilot. I'll choose the trip we'll be taking with your help. Sometimes you can steer; mostly you'll be in charge of the gas pedal and the brake. It's up to you to decide how fast or how slow we go to do this work together. I may nudge you a little bit, but you always have the power to put on the brakes.

Making sense of what happened requires children to revisit the trauma; this means opening the door to strong emotions. The counselor must act as a trusted guide and have the child examine these emotions in manageable doses after he or she has developed skills in containment and self-soothing.

Have the child create a story about what has happened. As counseling progresses, the story will change. The goal is for the child to have a story about the trauma that he or she understands at the proper developmental age—even though it may have frightening parts. The story-making will also allow the child to alter distorted beliefs about what happened. As the story changes, through step-by-step revisits of the event, it will become one in which the child can learn not to self-blame. The old parts of the story that contain self-blame can be changed so that the story includes, "What happened was not my fault." This revision helps the child regain self-confidence. Through the story-making, the learned terror and helplessness is unconditioned or unlearned.

Parents or caretakers must be engaged in the treatment process so that they can anticipate the child's emotional reactions and have tools for helping. To challenge the powerlessness and terror of the past requires the therapist to match strategy with the child's developmental age, internal resources, and style of emotional expression, as well as with family resources (especially important). For example, if a child likes to draw, use drawing to communicate the experience. Regularly review the artwork and discuss with the child how the drawings and the child's perceptions are changing. Other children may be more interested in keeping a journal to record high and low points of each day, to keep a list of coping skills they have learned, and to write new parts of their "story."

If a child likes to work with the sand tray or with figures in a dollhouse, listen for the underlying themes of traumatic play, and then become a codirector. Help the child transform the scene so that he or she acquires power, tries new choices, and gains mastery over the experience. For example, Andrea, the five-year-old who had been molested by a daycare worker, always had a witch in her sand tray stories. While sitting next to Andrea and watching her story, the therapist suggested ways that Andrea could gain power and escape. The therapist asked, "Andrea, how can you change what's happening? What about asking for help?" Andrea decided to call 911. She added a big policeman to the sand tray. Later she led all the children out of the fenced yard away from the witch. In other sessions, Andrea made witches out of clay and then squashed them and drew pictures of witches and then colored over each drawing with loud, heavy colors so that the witches disappeared.

The goal of any play therapy technique is for the child to understand what happened, to regain power, and to know that the trauma was not his or her fault. After any emotional play, end the session with a closing ritual that emphasizes quieting and closure.

Coordinate system intervention. If a child has been placed in a foster family or with relatives, the therapist needs to identify the key caretakers and to include them in the treatment process. A cooperative alliance needs to be built between the therapist and the adults involved in the care of the traumatized child. A regular, direct exchange describing the child's behavior at home and at school should take place between caretakers and therapists, via either the telephone or written notes. Caretakers need to be alerted to possible emotional and behavioral reactions when the child revisits the trauma during therapy. Educate the at-home adult about a child's alarm reaction, and teach the adult ways in which he or she can decrease this reaction and moderate intense feelings.

What Parents Can Do

Parents are also traumatized by what has happened to their child. They, too, experience feelings of helplessness, vulnerability, loss of safety, and loss of control. Encourage parents to find support for themselves so that they can continue to be strong, effective parents for their wounded child. Formal support can be found in groups associated with clinics, mental health centers, churches, or counselors—or informal, such as support from friends. If the parents do not have support, the risk is that parents will feel overwhelmed, confused, and powerless, and that the chhild will feel even more vulnerable. Parents must be encouraged not to minimize the trauma or try to forget that it happened.

Invite the parents to stay involved in their child's counseling process. Give them homework assignments to practice between sessions such as relaxation exercises, anger expression, storytelling, and sitting alongside their child during pretend play. Also encourage them to do fun, relaxing activities together regularly, such as listening to music, watching movies and videos, reading a book aloud, playing games, bicycling, or hiking.

The parents have the difficult task of communicating with the legal system, victim's compensation, social services, or insurance companies. These tasks can also be traumatic. Again, encourage parents to have a support person or group that can listen to their frustrations, anger, or shame and help problem-solve. Many victim compensation services (public service agencies that are part of the judicial system and are housed within the district attorney's office) have an advocate whose job it is to be an ally for the parents.

Remember to prepare parents for the impact of the one-year anniversary of the event. During this time, the reactions of the child may be intense and difficult, but will usually be brief. Also advise parents that when a child enters a new developmental stage, symptoms may return. A classic example is a child who is sexually abused during preschool and who, when he or she begins puberty, may exhibit exaggerated sexualized behaviors that necessitates brief treatment.

What Teachers Can Do

Teachers can provide a safe, consistent environment where children can successfully learn, play, and be with friends, a place where they can leave their trauma behind for part of each day. Lenore Terr reports in her book *Too Scared to Cry* that many traumatized children continue to do well in school. These are children who are able to cope by focusing on schoolwork. Other children, however, are still in the alarm state and unable to sustain focus.

If the child has a positive relationship with his or her teacher, and if the child is willing, encourage the parents to inform the teacher about the trauma the child has experienced. Sometimes parents are reluctant to divulge this information because they want to protect the privacy of their child. Get the parents' permission to talk at least by phone with the teacher, and be sure to describe the post-traumatic alarm state experienced by the child. If the child is chronically in a heightened state of fear, he or she may have difficulty learning.

Ask the teacher to describe any changes in behavior, peer relationships, or academic performance. If the child is misbehaving or appears distracted in the classroom, the teacher may think the child is purposely being difficult or is exhibiting symptoms of ADHD. Ask whether the child is daydreaming and/or not completing assignments. Explain that these are also symptoms of Post-traumatic Stress Disorder. If the child does show stress at school, encourage the teacher to temporarily lower academic expectations, and to provide extra encouragement, positive support, and structure. It is often helpful for the school personnel to play an active part in the treatment plan for the child. It is valuable for the therapist to know whether the child's behavior at school is improving or regressing.

In situations involving child abuse, teachers are expected to know mandatory abuse-reporting laws in their state and school district. Every school district has a detailed policy outlining what a teacher must do if abuse is suspected. School is often the first place where abuse is suspected because a child confides in a friend or teacher or because of changes in the child's appearance and behavior. Remind teachers that the following signs may suggest abuse or trauma:

- verbal or written expressions of hopelessness or helplessness
- aggressive behavior, especially during recess
- sexualized play with peers
- premature understanding of such things as sexual behavior or sexual jokes
- masturbation in the classroom or during recess
- sexual themes in art and written work
- delinquent behaviors
- unusual and frequent stomachaches, headaches, or other somatic complaints
- lack of personal boundaries, such as hugging unfamiliar adults or seductive behavior with teachers
- a sudden decrease in academic performance.

These symptoms serve as warning signs that something is wrong in a child's life. Except for the sexual behaviors, other stressors, such as parental conflict, divorce, remarriage, death of a family member, parental alcoholism, or domestic violence could cause these symptoms. Stress to teachers that when they observe these behaviors, they should consider the possibility that something important may be worrying or upsetting the child, rather than assume the child is being bad, uncaring, or lazy.

COMMON ISSUES

There are some children for whom outpatient counseling is inappropriate as well as ineffective. These are:

- children who have been abused or severely neglected for years
- children who have basic attachment disorder
- children who have multiple problems such as significant developmental delays or other serious emotional disorders
- children who continue to live in an abusive or chaotic environment
- children who are exhibiting predatory behavior toward people or property.

Refer a child whose behavior is dangerous to self or others, a child who has rage episodes, or a child who is depressed to a child psychiatrist for evaluation and possible medication. If the self-destructive, aggressive, or rage behavior does not respond to medications or multimodal psychotherapy, residential treatment may be needed. Symptoms indicating that a client needs more than outpatient therapy include aggressive, destructive behaviors; behaviors provoking others to victimize the child; torture or killing of animals; compulsive lying; repetitive deliquent behaviors, especially stealing and vandalism; fire-setting; symptoms of psychosis; and escalating suicidal ideation.

The decision about residential treatment should be based on a complete psychological assessment. The therapist can begin this process by documenting the therapeutic strategies that have been tried, describing the frequency or severity of symptomatic behaviors, and then referring to a child psychologist or psychiatrist.

A common problem in treating traumatized children is the amount of required case management. A client who has been placed in protective custody will have a number of adults with whom a therapist needs to communicate and to consult. The child might have a social service case manager, foster parents, biological parents, and a legal representative. It is crucial to have a clear understanding of those with whom you share information.

MEASURING PROGRESS

Measure the therapeutic process regularly by first reviewing the list of traumagenic states. Note what states the child was experiencing at the beginning of treatment. Then identify what symptoms remain. For example, if the reason for counseling was problematic behavior, such as sexualized play, temper tantrums, or nightmares, then progress can be measured by observing the decrease in frequency and intensity of these symptoms. Finally, discuss with the child and parents the tasks mastered, the new skills learned, and what tasks still need mastering.

ANTICIPATED PROGRESS AND OUTCOMES

The child who experiences trauma is forever changed. The hope for healing is that the child will gain mastery and make sense of the overwhelming experience. (It is interesting that the Japanese symbol for crisis incorporates both danger and opportunity.) Traumatized children feel helplessness and terror, and yet they gain power by surviving. With guidance, they can learn that what happened to them is not their fault. They can regain confidence in their strengths and abilities. They also can learn that not all adults are trustworthy or safe, but that most are. Healing children understand that many events are beyond their control and that self-blame and guilt are unnecessary. These children can once again learn to play and to be childlike, happy, silly, and loving.

RESOURCES
Books for Parents, Teachers, and Counselors

Allan, J. *Inscapes of the Child's World.* Dallas, TX: Spring Publications, 1988.

Many examples of children's drawings, pictures of sand trays, and case studies. A powerful reference for counselors who use art therapy and the sand tray as treatment.

Burgess, A., ed. *Childhood Trauma: Issues and Research.* New York, NY: Garland Publishers, 1992.

A collection of current research articles on childhood trauma, treatment options, and future implications.

Capacchione, L. *Creative Journaling for Children.* Boston, MA: Shambhala Press, 1989.

Strategies to encourage children to use language to express thoughts and feelings.

Davis, N. *Once Upon a Time... Therapeutic Stories for Abused Children.* Oxon Hill, MD: Psychological Associates, 1990.

A collection of metaphorical stories that are useful in treating children and families with a variety of problems.

Day, J. *Creative Visualization.* Rockport, MA: Element, Inc., 1994.

How to teach visualization techniques to children.

Friedrich, W. *Psychotherapy of Sexually Abused Children and Their Families.* New York, NY: W. W. Norton Co., 1990.

Comprehensive summary of treatment issues.

Gil, E. *The Healing Power of Play: Working with Abused Children.* New York, NY: Guilford Press, 1991.

Important reference for the child therapist. Concrete descriptions and six detailed case studies. Especially good summary of sexualized play in traumatized children.

"Invincible Kids." *U. S. News & World Report.* November 11, 1996, pp. 62-74.

A collection of stories based on research on childhood trauma; includes research on what helped children heal. For parents and counselors.

James, B. *Treating Traumatized Chidren.* Lexington, MA: Lexington Books/D. C. Heath, 1989.

Many readable and practical strategies; comprehensive.

Linesch, D. Art *Therapy with Families in Crisis.* New York, NY: Brunner/Mazel, 1993.

Describes many practical exercises that facilitate nonverbal communication about painful topics.

Mills, J., R. Crowley, and M. O'Ryan. *Therapeutic Metaphors for Children and the Child Within.* New York, NY: Brunner/Mazel, 1986.
How to use storytelling to heal traumatized children.

Murdock, M. *Spinning Inward.* Boston, MA: Shambhala Press, 1989.
Many exercises for guided imagery to use with children of all ages.

Oaklander, V. *Windows into Our Children.* New York, NY: W. W. Norton &

Co., Inc., 1988.

Classic resource for techniques to use with children.

Terr, L. *Too Scared to Cry.* New York, NY: Basic Books.

Provides the therapist and other concerned adults with an understanding of the emotional changes in traumatized children. The focus is not on treatment.

Books for Children

Garth, M. *Starbright and Moonbright.* New York, NY: HarperCollins, 1995.

Short, imaginary trips for a parent or a counselor to read with a traumatized child. Book includes imagery such as a worry tree, a secret garden, and an angel.

Hindman, J. *A Touching Book.* Ontario, OR: Alexandria Associates, 1990.

Addresses good, bad, and secret touching. Helps children seven and younger talk about appropriate touching and guides them through what to do if someone touches them inappropriately. Humorous but realistic illustrations.

Lankton, S. *The Blammo-Surprise Book.* New York, NY: Magination Press, 1988.

The story of how one child learns to overcome his fears by replacing them with strong, positive feelings. For all children of school age.

Lobby, T. *Jessica and the Bad Wolf.* New York, NY: Magination Press, 1990.

Demonstrates a practical strategy for parents to help a child having nightmares. Small picturebook.

Millman, D. *Secret of the Peaceful Warrior.* Thornton, CA: Starseed Press, 1991.

An inspirational story about courage and the nonviolent ways to approach a bully. Recommended for all children and especially helpful to traumatized children. Benjamin Franklin Award winner.

Olofsdotter, M. *Sofia and the Heartmender.* Minneapolis, MN: Free Spirit Press, 1995.

For the child ages five and older. The story of the healing of a broken heart. First Place, Best Children's Book, Mid-American Publishers Association.

Paterson, K. *The Great Gilly Hopkins.* New York, NY: Scholastic, 1995.

Fiction. An eleven-year-old girl in a foster home tries to cope with her fears and hopes.

Agencies and Organizations

Magination Press
750 First St., NE
Washington, D.C. 20002-4242
(800) 374- 2721

Publishing company. Specializes in illustrated books written by professionals. For the younger child; helps parents help their children.

Interpersonal Violence—The Practice Series
John R. Conte, editor
Sage Publications
2455 Teller Road
Thousand Oaks, CA 91320

A series devoted to professionals who work with survivors of personal violence.

National Association of Crime Victim Compensation Boards
Dan Eddy, Executive Director
P. O. Box 16003
Alexandria, VA 22302
(703) 370-2996

Local compensation boards help crime victims get financial aid and therapeutic referrals.

Index

Mutual Storytelling Techniques, 10, 32
one-on-one time, 31
Owens Behavior Checklist, 93
Peabody Individual Achievement Test, 81
Personality Inventory for Children (PIC), 93
play therapy, 46, 49, 166
Post-traumatic Stress Disorder (PTSD), 49, 153, 154, 168
projective techniques, 4, 27
Report on Gifted Children and Education, 89
relaxation techniques, 13, 47
Reynolds Adolescent Depression Inventory, 43, 113
Reynolds Child Depression Inventory, 5, 43, 157
rosebush technique, 4, 114, 158
school failure, 130
school phobia, 80
self-portrait, 158
social skills training, 142
solution-focused therapy, 32
Stepfamilies/Blended Families, 23-40
    assessment, 27-30
    behavioral indicators, 27-28
    biological parents, 34
    change in birth order, 26
    common issues, 35-36
    developmental considerations, 28-30
    divided loyalties, 25
    dynamics, 24
    emotional tasks of stepchildren, 24
    intervention strategies, 30-35
        for counselors, 30-33
        for parents, 34-35
        for teachers, 35
    key issues, 27-28
    new siblings, 25
    progress, signs of, 36
    physical affection, 35
    resources, 37-40
        agencies/ organizations, 40
        for adults, 37-39

Notes